The Michigan Divorce and Child Custody Handbook

The Michigan Divorce and Child Custody Handbook

A PRACTICAL INTRODUCTION

Thomas C. Kates, JD

ISBN: 0692611983
ISBN 13: 9780692611982
Library of Congress Control Number: 2016900030
Thomas C. Kates, Attorney and Mediator, Holland, MI

For Jennifer

Table of Contents

Disclaimer

As you read this book, please remember a few important things. First, no two divorces are the same, and the law is constantly changing. Nothing contained in this book should be construed as legal advice regarding your particular situation. This book should not be considered a substitute for a relationship with an attorney. No attorney-client relationship is created by your reading this book. Much of what is written here is opinion, based on my personal experience as a family law attorney. I will be the first to tell you that I do not have all of the answers. I have worked with many attorneys, and while we all must operate within the confines of the law, no two attorneys do things exactly alike. I have no doubt that, if your attorney reads this book, he or she may disagree with some of my assertions. If something in this book contradicts what your attorney has told you, by all means bring that to your attorney's attention but follow his or her advice. The opinions and information contained in this book should serve as a starting point for discussions with your attorney and enable you to ask the pertinent questions as you work together.

Thomas C. Kates

Introduction

"Never in a million years did I think I'd
find myself in this position."

Countless people who come to my law office for their first divorce consultation say this to me. While divorce is commonplace in our society, few of us marry contemplating that we may be among the unfortunate percentage of people whose marriages end that way. So we throw ourselves into marriage with our whole hearts and march forward through the years hand-in-hand, accumulating assets and personal possessions, incurring debt, and passing on our shared values to our children, all the while never contemplating that one day it may end bitterly when the divorce papers are served. As we realize our marriage is ending, we experience intense emotions, including grief, shock, anger and confusion. We may feel alone and abandoned, vulnerable even in our own homes. And on top of the intense emotion, we face an array of practical challenges and the reality that the marital estate will be split in two through an emotionally devastating, expensive and all-consuming process.

This book will serve as a guide to those facing divorce in the state of Michigan. Whether you are unsure if you will be divorcing or are in the late stages of negotiating your divorce settlement, this book will provide practical advice to lessen the mystique surrounding the process, cut through the legal jargon and provide a greater understanding of the way attorneys work. It will explain the legal standards for divorce, custody and related issues, and help you prepare for divorce negotiations or trial. In addition, if you heed this book's advice you will become a savvier consumer of legal services.

Because of the high emotional stakes, if you are facing divorce I urge you to establish a relationship with a counseling professional experienced in helping people cope with the grief, trauma and anxiety that inevitably accompany divorce. Even the healthiest people will experience these emotions to some degree. While your relationship with a counselor is beyond the scope of this book, I cannot overstate the importance of obtaining emotional support. Before you divorce, a mental health professional can assist you in sorting through other viable options and help you determine whether there is any likelihood that your marriage can be preserved. This process may take months, or even years.

No two marriages are exactly alike, nor are any two divorces. Some of the advice in this book may simply not apply to your situation. You will notice that much of the discussion centers on finding amicable resolutions. By now you may be thinking to yourself, *Amicable? Apparently this guy has never met my spouse!* It is true that in some divorces amicable resolution is virtually impossible. If you just found out yesterday that your husband has been engaged in 14 different extramarital affairs and infected you with a variety of sexually transmitted diseases, or has liquidated his 401(k) to pay gambling debts, the word *amicable* is most likely absent from your vocabulary at the moment. But before you put this book back on the shelf, rest assured that an understanding of the divorce process will assist you greatly, whether your divorce is one that is amenable to quick resolution or, at the other end of the spectrum, a contentious battle that will continue for years to come.

Whatever your situation, I am confident that if you develop a basic understanding of divorce law and procedure, you will experience a more economical and efficient divorce, enabling you and your soon-to-be ex-spouse to devote your energies to healing financially and emotionally, allowing you both to move on with your lives in a productive manner. Regardless of your age, educational level or financial status, an understanding of the process and knowledge of what to expect as you navigate the uncharted waters ahead will spare you and your family unnecessary emotional and financial stress.

CHAPTER 1

How Do We Tell the Children?

> "Each day of our lives we make deposits in
> the memory banks of our children."
> — CHARLES SWINDOLL

t was winter semester 1981. As I trudged across campus through the building snowdrifts, backpack slung over my shoulder, there came a familiar voice. "Tom," he called out. "Hey, Kates!" I looked over my shoulder just as my old high school buddy, now living a floor above me in the dorm, loped toward me through the knee-deep snow.

"Tom, I was really sorry to hear the news Sunday in church. How are your folks doing?"

I stopped and turned toward him. "Ok, I guess. News? What are you talking about?"

"You know, your grandma—she—she died, right? At least that's what they said at church. I was home for the weekend. I guess you must've stayed on campus." He kicked a chunk of ice with the toe of his sneaker and pushed up his coat sleeve to look at his watch.

"I guess I must be the last one to know about these things. I had no idea," I said.

"Oh man, I'm sorry. I figured you'd know by now. It's been like a week," he said. "Anyway, guess I'd better get to class. I'll see ya around."

"Yeah, thanks," I called out as he trotted away through the snow.

A college sophomore and far from an expert in communication, even I sensed something terribly wrong with this exchange. To this day I wonder why my parents did not simply call and tell me that my grandmother was dead. Was it simply too painful? Did they think they were sheltering me from something upsetting? Had they just forgotten about me in their emotional distress or did they not care about my feelings? As I stood there that bleak winter day, on top of deep sadness at the realization that my grandma was gone, I felt confused, angry, and alone.

It may seem elementary, but when it comes to breaking the news of a pending divorce to your children, I say just tell them. My advice would be that the worst course of action is to do nothing at all. Of course, you may want to time the event to avoid a birthday or holiday, but do not delay just because it is difficult. In this day and age, there is a good chance your child will learn the devastating news through social media or other indirect channels, which is reason enough to tell your children sooner rather than later.

Before you tell your children of a pending divorce, be sure to consult with a mental health professional who can assist you in handling the matter in a way that will minimize the traumatic effect on your children. Of equal importance, remember that you will not tell your children about your divorce only once. You will have continued opportunities to answer questions as your children grow older. I recommend that you make the children aware of what is happening in an age-appropriate fashion as soon as you are certain the divorce will happen and, of course, if you are the one initiating it, after your spouse is aware. I recommend that if you can do it peaceably, the two of you meet with the children to present a consistent portrayal of the situation.

There are a few key things to remember when talking about divorce with children. First, it is important to put to rest any misconceptions the child might have concerning his or her own fault in causing the breakdown of the marriage, especially in the case of younger children. If tension has been building in the household in the days leading up to the divorce, a child may come to see the divorce as something he or she has caused. It is important to dispel this belief as soon as possible, and there is no better way to do this than to arrange professional counseling for your child. Some communities offer divorce recovery classes for children through local churches or mental health organizations. These classes can help children deal with the confusion, grief and anger that often accompany their parents' divorce. Check with the Friend of the Court office for a list of opportunities and enroll your child in whatever you feel is appropriate as soon as possible.

Second, recognize that no matter what your child learns in a divorce recovery class or through individual counseling, your demeanor toward your soon-to-be ex-spouse is the most important factor in helping your child to adjust. As discussed below, no matter how hurt or angry you may feel, you must not let your personal emotions get in the way of your child's relationship with the other parent. Strive to teach your children that while your family may be going through significant and often very painful changes, you are still a family. Your children need to hear that, although you and your spouse will no longer be husband and wife, you will still continue to love and care for them. They need to understand that you are committed to continue working as a team with the other parent to see that all their needs are met. If a child is old enough to understand the concept of a business partnership, this can be a helpful illustration. Business partners do not necessarily need to be close friends, but if they are to succeed, they must have a cordial, open and honest relationship, where responsibilities are shared. Most children can understand this analogy.

Do not share the specifics of the divorce with the children any more than they need to understand simply that Mom and Dad will not be married anymore. If there has been substance abuse, domestic violence or other frightening stuff going on, children will likely understand the role this may play in their parents' separation, and you may not need to say much at all. If there are more subtle but equally destructive behaviors involved, such as addictions or infidelity, the children will likely find out about these as they grow older, and I see no reason to discuss these issues with them, especially when they are very young.

I suggest that you discuss the specifics of your situation, preferably together, with a mental health professional, before saying anything to the children.

However, do not put it off simply because it is uncomfortable. You do not want your children to find out through a third party. That will only contribute to the feelings of confusion and grief they will undoubtedly experience. Telling them in a frank, honest and hopeful way is the first step toward helping them recover.

CHAPTER 2

How To Team Up With A Great Divorce Attorney
and Make the Most of the Relationship

"As a peacemaker the lawyer has a superior opportunity of
being a good man. There will still be business enough."
— ABRAHAM LINCOLN

Do I Really Need an Attorney?

As divorce looms on the horizon, people face the first of many crucial decisions: Will it be necessary to retain an attorney and if so, what is the best way to find one? At this stage, one may be hit with a barrage of advice from well-meaning friends and relatives, ranging from admonishments that divorce is wrong and no matter what the person is enduring, marriage is for life to providing attorney referrals in hopes the family member will find the toughest, most cutthroat attorney on the planet and really take the S.O.B. to the cleaners. This well-meaning advice tends to only heighten one's feelings of confusion and ambivalence.

One question my clients commonly ask is whether they can handle their own divorce without an attorney. At the risk of sounding self-serving, I respond that while the law does not require anyone to have an attorney to go to court, and it is possible to proceed unrepresented, it is highly preferable to team up with an experienced attorney to guide a person through the confusing and complex process of divorce. In certain circumstances, people are able to proceed unrepresented with some success. However, this is the exception, rather than the rule. I have seen individuals with extremely limited assets and no children, or with highly amicable parenting relationships, handle their own divorces, sometimes with assistance of a county legal self-help center, with a fair and equitable outcome. However, more often than not, when an individual comes to my office after a divorce where neither party was represented, or worse yet, where one party had an attorney and the other proceeded without one, the outcome is unfairly skewed, or to some degree unworkable, necessitating costly remedial measures after the judgment has entered. Ultimately, the damage that can be done through attempting to represent oneself is more expensive to remediate than the cost of retaining counsel at the outset.

That being said, if you simply do not have enough money to retain an attorney, or if you have modest assets and custody of your children is not at issue, you may be able to handle the paperwork and negotiations on your own. Many counties have legal self-help centers with a library of forms available for the *pro se* litigant. With a little business savvy and some study, some people are able to resolve their divorces without setting foot in an attorney's office. If you are ready to take on this challenge, at the very least you should find a resource guide for the unrepresented individual. One helpful book I recommend is *The Michigan Divorce Book, a Guide to Doing an Uncontested Divorce Without an Attorney,* by Michael Maran (Lansing, Michigan: Grand River Press), available in most libraries and bookstores. It is an excellent resource containing divorce forms, a basic explanation of the law and a roadmap for handling uncontested divorces. While the book offers invaluable information, as the author freely states, it should not serve as a substitute for a relationship with a knowledgeable attorney.

My advice to you would be this: Unless you fall into the category of extremely simple divorces described above or if you absolutely cannot afford an attorney, you should retain one, and the sooner the better.

With All the Attorneys Out There, How Can I Find One I Can Trust?

Lawyers—and many of them—can be found in virtually every county in Michigan. As of 2013, the American Bar Association Market Research Department estimated there were approximately 34,000 resident and active attorneys in Michigan. While there is no shortage of legal talent here, in most cases the sheer number of attorneys makes choosing which one to retain more difficult.

When looking for a divorce attorney, find one with substantial specialized experience in family law. In doing so, first understand that anyone can hold oneself out as a specialist in any area of law simply by saying so. Beware of the lawyer who holds himself out as specializing, for example, in divorce, custody, personal injury, bankruptcy, estate planning, criminal law and general civil litigation. Clearly, this lawyer specializes in nothing at all and is simply trying to survive by handling any legal matter that comes through the door. Avoid the "Jack of all trades" lawyer, no matter what the advertisements may say.

There are many ways to find a lawyer. Having watched many people pick their way through the masses of lawyers eager to render services, I have come to believe that the most effective way to find a trustworthy and capable attorney is by referral from individuals who have utilized the lawyer's services in the past. There will likely be people in your workplace, place of worship, or civic organization who have divorced in recent years. Most people are willing to share their experiences and opinions, good or bad, of their divorce. If you are fortunate enough to know a few people who have recently divorced, ask a couple if they are willing to share their experiences over a cup of coffee. You need not get into the specifics of their case. Just ask a few open-ended questions, such as "How was your experience with Mary when you went through your divorce?" or "Did you find John's fees to be reasonable?" You will in most cases hear honest appraisals of the attorney's abilities, trustworthiness, and the overall experience. If you receive an opinion, good or bad, from an individual you trust, give it some consideration, but do not proceed to select a lawyer solely on one person's viewpoint. Ask people how they became involved with the lawyer.

They may give you the names of others who know him or her. People tend to have very strong opinions about attorneys, whether positive or negative. Most people are eager to talk about their experience, especially if it was negative.

Once you have received a personal recommendation, preferably corroborated by a second or third person, take time to research the attorney and the law firm by reviewing the firm's website if there is one and, of equal importance, searching other resources online. Pay close attention to the attorney's years in practice and areas of specialization. How long has she been practicing? Has the attorney authored articles on family law? Has she been involved in any professional organizations evidencing involvement in the family law community? Be wary of the attorney who tells you he is a specialist in family law, but the only thing he has ever written about is bankruptcy or environmental litigation. Is she on the board of any organizations that establish credibility in the community?

Pay attention to both the good and bad online buzz about the lawyer you are researching. Does the attorney have a blog, and if so, is it dedicated to family law, or does it discuss every area of law from dog bites to drunk driving? A family law specialist will display specialized knowledge in a blog if she has one. If the lawyer tells you he specializes in family law but spends all his time blogging about personal injury, his credibility should be suspect. I have heard lawyers say they will handle divorces "to keep the lights on" while they try to develop other practice areas. You should avoid lawyers with this attitude. Family law is a practice area that requires unique personality traits not all lawyers possess. Chances are if a lawyer is handling divorces just because he cannot find any other work, he will not give your divorce case the attention it deserves.

The State Bar of Michigan maintains a database of attorneys who have been subject to professional disciplinary proceedings. If an attorney has been disciplined for neglecting a legal proceeding, for misappropriation of client funds, or for criminal behavior, you can learn the specifics of this by researching the database. You will also find that many attorneys have been reviewed online by clients on websites such as *Yahoo!, Google, Yelp, Avvo and Yellow Pages*. While these reviews may be helpful, keep in mind that anyone can review an attorney, and even attorneys with stellar reputations may have a bad review or two on their online profile, possibly from a disgruntled client who had unreasonable expectations to begin with. Not everyone is pleased with the ultimate outcome of their divorce proceeding, and it is not always reasonable to blame the attorney. Look at the overall trend of online reviews. If the feedback is overwhelmingly positive, you can probably ignore the occasional angry criticism. But if negativity is the trend, perhaps you should avoid the lawyer.

If you are active in your community, chances are that you have social or business contacts with lawyers. For example, if you serve on a board with a lawyer, you have seen him in action and can independently assess his level of trustworthiness, business savvy, and communication skills. If he does not practice family law, ask to whom he refers such clients. This is an excellent source of information, as lawyers are well aware of the reputations of their colleagues. They are putting their own reputations on the line with their clients when they refer them to other lawyers, so wise practitioners will only refer clients to lawyers they trust.

Relying on a lawyer's advertising, whether online or in the telephone directory, should be a last resort. However, if you are unable to receive a personal recommendation for a lawyer, online or print advertisements can be a starting point. Review a lawyer's advertising carefully. Does the lawyer claim to specialize in family law as opposed to saying "We are a full-service law firm"? If the lawyer does not have an online presence, it may be a sign he or she has not been practicing for long. In Michigan, you can tell how many years a lawyer has been in practice by his or her "P number". This is the five digit number preceded by the letter P that always appears after a lawyer's signature on court documents. Those with a P number beginning with 1 have as a rule been practicing 40 years or more. The higher the number, the less experienced the lawyer. Lawyers admitted to practice in the past decade have numbers roughly 7000 or greater. There are some exceptions, such as when a lawyer previously licensed in a different state comes to Michigan later in his career. In those cases, a high P number will not necessarily signify an inexperienced lawyer.

Whether you are fortunate enough to have found enthusiastic endorsements of your prospective lawyer from those you trust or are simply going on what is stated in the phone book or other advertising sources, take time to personally interview the lawyer before making a hiring decision. Look at the initial consultation as a job interview, and do not hesitate to advise the lawyer when you call for your first appointment that you are interviewing lawyers and have not yet decided who you will retain. In many cases, lawyers do not charge for the initial interview. Expect this meeting to last 30 minutes or so. At this meeting the lawyer should discuss his or her credentials with you, hear a little about your case, and allow you to make a hiring decision.

If you hope to spend an hour or two picking the lawyer's brain about every aspect of your case, make that clear when you schedule the appointment, and expect to pay a fee. When you call the lawyer's office, be sure to ask about fees for the initial consultation. Some lawyers will gladly sit with you for an hour and even give you specific advice, without a fee. Others, generally those who are busier and perhaps more in demand, will not so much as talk to you on the phone without a fee. Whatever the arrangement, you have the right to know in advance what it is going to cost. If you have received a good recommendation, do not be deterred by an initial consultation fee, as it is money well spent in most cases.

Once you have arranged your initial consultation, prepare to interview the lawyer to find out whether she has the experience you are looking for and whether your personalities are a good fit. At a minimum, ask the following questions:

- How long have you been practicing law? (If less than five or 10 years, this is not a deal-breaker, but proceed with caution.)
- What percentage of your caseload is devoted to family law? (I would not be comfortable with anything less than 50%.)
- Do you practice in _____ County? What percentage of your caseload is there? (Depending on your region, the lawyer should demonstrate a significant portion of family law practice in the county where you reside, as each county has procedures unique to the jurisdiction and a lawyer unfamiliar with those is at a disadvantage.)
- How many divorce cases do you currently have open?
- What is your hourly fee and do you require a retainer up front?

- What is your philosophy on settling cases versus going to trial?
- Are you a fighter? (As discussed below, this is a loaded question, and if the lawyer says unabashedly yes, in my opinion, he should be avoided, at least in family law cases, and especially where children are involved.)
- Do you like practicing family law, and if not, what areas of law do you prefer?
- What is your opinion of the judges in _____ County? (Beware the judge-bashing lawyer. This may be a sign that the lawyer does not have a good track record with one or more judges.)
- If I hire you as my attorney, will you be doing the work yourself or delegating it to someone else? (Some attorneys will sign up clients based on their track record and experience, only to delegate the work to inexperienced associates. If you are hiring a particular attorney based on his experience, make it clear that you expect him to personally appear in court unless otherwise agreed.)
- Does your firm charge for work done by paralegals, legal assistants or secretaries, and if so, what is the hourly rate for each?
- Do you charge for postage, photocopies, etc.?
- How do you feel about mediation? Do you ever serve as a mediator? (Because nearly all cases are now referred to mediation in most counties, if your lawyer is not in favor of mediation, the process may not work for you. If a lawyer commonly serves as a mediator for other family law cases, it is a good indicator of expertise, and also may reveal that the lawyer is a good communicator and trusted by her colleagues.)
- How many cases do you win? (Again, this is a bit of a trick question, but one that should be asked. If the lawyer tells you that he always wins, proceed with caution. In my opinion, the proper answer is that no one ever really wins in family law cases, but the lawyer's objective should be to achieve an equitable outcome, and a resolution that is in the best interest of the children. If the lawyer makes guarantees, or tells you that your case is a "sure thing", or "an open and shut case", perhaps he is not being honest with you. A good lawyer will tell you some things you do not want to hear.)

As you interview the prospective lawyer using the above questions as a guide, observe him carefully. Is he comfortable with your inquiries or does he appear to squirm? Does he seem to take your matter seriously and appear to want to be your attorney? Does she appear impatient or rushed? Is he texting or taking phone calls during the interview? Is she a good listener or do you feel as though her primary purpose is to inflate your perception of her through self-aggrandizing war stories that have nothing to do with your case? Is the office well-organized and appropriately staffed?

Don't be taken aback if you ask a question and don't get the answer you want to hear. For instance, sometimes clients will ask me something like "Since my husband has been cheating on me, I feel like the court should teach him a lesson and never let him see the kids again. Can you make that happen?" In such cases a good lawyer will explain how the law treats such situations and attempt to educate the client on the likely outcomes rather than feeding the client's unreasonable expectations or vindictive motives. A tactful practitioner might respond to such an inquiry by stating: "The fact of the matter is, Susan, Mark is still the children's dad and unless he has a track record of abuse or inappropriate behaviors that affect the children, the court will not deprive him of the right to spend time with the kids. The judge needs to look at what is in their best interests, and punishment of the unfaithful spouse is not one of the criteria the courts use. This is how our custody laws work and I know Judge Jones adheres to this standard in custody cases." A good lawyer will deliver an honest assessment with tact and not make a potential client feel like a complete idiot for asking such a question. She will teach a client about the law along the way. While it is important that you team up with a lawyer who can advocate strongly for your position, keep in mind that regardless of what the lawyer says or does, the judge, if he is a good one, will decide the case based on the law.

If you get the feeling that your personalities click, take things a bit further and ask for an in-depth analysis of your case. At this phase of the relationship the lawyer should be asking numerous questions exploring, for example, your perception of the breakdown of the marriage relationship and your desired outcome. Is the attorney willing and able to listen to you or does she need to do all the talking? What are the issues or problems that led you to seek divorce counsel? Does the attorney say things that lead you to believe she will be a diplomatic negotiator, or does she gratuitously bash the competition? An effective lawyer will have a businesslike and professional attitude toward opposing counsel. If you know who your spouse's attorney will be, share this with the attorney and gauge his reaction.

Ask him if he is a fighter. This in my opinion is a loaded question. Whether he says yes or no, ask him to explain. This will tell you if the attorney is one who will work diplomatically to find a practical solution or up the ante by filing unnecessary motions that serve only to escalate the conflict and the resulting fees.

If you have a good feeling about the attorney after the initial meeting, ask about fees. As discussed below, this should be a frank and open discussion. Don't leave the first appointment without a clear understanding of hourly rates and any required retainer and upfront costs, as this is an important element of your hiring decision. Once you have this information, give it a day or two before you commit. Talk to someone you trust about your impressions of the lawyer and process your thoughts. If you feel uncomfortable or unsure of the decision, it never hurts to repeat the process a second or third time with another lawyer, preferably one recommended by a trusted source. Take careful notes during the interviews so your thought process will be organized as you come to a decision on who your attorney will be. This may be the most important decision you make as you move through the divorce process.

The Attorney-Client Relationship

Now that you have decided to retain a particular attorney, it's time for some in-depth conversation concerning your goals and desired outcome. At a minimum, you should convey to your attorney your expectations in the areas discussed below. This conversation should occur at your first or second meeting, preferably prior to the divorce papers being filed if you are the plaintiff or prior to your attorney filing an answer on your behalf if you are the defendant. You should leave this meeting with a clear understanding of your objectives, and hopefully you will feel confident that your attorney is on the same page with you.

- Domestic violence concerns. Your attorney should discuss with you in the initial meeting whether you have at any time felt unsafe or threatened. If so, this can change the tenor of the entire case and there are certain precautions that need to be taken at the outset. (See chapter 9 on domestic violence below.)
- Custody of minor children and parenting time. If you have children under 18 years old (or in the case of a child who does not graduate from high school until he is older, this can be age 19½) custody must be addressed. Let your attorney know what you hope to achieve and what you believe your spouse's response will be. Then ask the attorney for an honest assessment of your position. It is important to determine at the outset whether custody will be contested or agreed upon. Your attorney can also run a support analysis under the Michigan Child Support Formula to give you an idea of what child support will look like.
- Property settlement. What do you hope to receive in the final settlement? In Michigan the rule of law is that property is to be divided *equitably*, which in most cases means equally, but not always. Give your attorney as much information as you can regarding what is owned by you and your spouse and the origin and value of the assets.
- Spousal support (alimony). Spousal support is based largely on length of the marriage and relative earnings of the parties. Early in your case your lawyer should look at your and your spouse's income information to run the Michigan Spousal Support Guidelines and provide a ballpark analysis of what you might reasonably expect to pay or receive as alimony.
- Real property. If you own a home or other real estate this may be divided between you and your spouse. Ask your attorney to recommend an appraiser.

- Debts. Be sure to give your attorney a complete itemization of all debts, whether incurred prior to or during the marriage. I always advise my clients to run a credit check on themselves and, with proper authorization, on the spouse and provide me a copy.
- Retirement assets. If possible, obtain recent statements for all IRAs, 401(k) accounts, pension plans or other retirement assets. If you or your spouse had any retirement accounts prior to the marriage, try to find statements for those accounts from at or near the date of the marriage.

While all of the above issues should be discussed early in the divorce proceeding, in most cases the attorney will need more information before she can provide an in-depth analysis of the probable outcome of the case. The more information you provide in your initial meeting, the more readily your attorney can analyze foreseeable outcomes and develop a strategy for settlement or trial.

The attorney-client relationship is characterized by a high degree of confidence, trust and confidentiality. The responsibilities owed by an attorney to the client are summarized in the Preamble to Comment following Rule 1.0 of the Michigan Rules of Professional Conduct:

A lawyer is a representative of clients, an officer of the legal system and a public citizen having special responsibility for the quality of justice.

As a representative of clients, a lawyer performs various functions. As advisor, a lawyer provides a client with an informed understanding of the client's legal rights and obligations and explains their practical implications. As advocate, a lawyer zealously asserts the client's position under the rules of the adversary system. As negotiator, a lawyer seeks a result advantageous to the client but consistent with requirements of honest dealing with others. As intermediary between clients, a lawyer seeks to reconcile their divergent interests as an advisor and, to a limited extent, as a spokesperson for each client. A lawyer acts as evaluator by examining a client's legal affairs and reporting about them to the client or to others.

In all professional functions a lawyer should be competent, prompt and diligent. A lawyer should maintain communication with a client concerning the representation. A lawyer should keep in confidence information relating to representation of a client except so far as disclosure is required or permitted by the Rules of Professional Conduct or other law.

A lawyer's conduct should conform to the requirements of the law, both in professional service to clients and in the lawyer's business and personal affairs. A lawyer should use the law's procedures only for legitimate purposes and not to harass or intimidate others. A lawyer should demonstrate respect for the legal system and for those who serve it, including judges, other lawyers and public officials. While it is a lawyer's duty, when necessary, to challenge the rectitude of official action, it is also a lawyer's duty to uphold legal process. (MRCP 1.0, Preamble to Comment)

As your case progresses, be mindful of the above duties incumbent upon your lawyer. If at any time you feel your lawyer is not conforming to the Rules of Professional Conduct, bring these concerns to your attorney's attention immediately. The legal profession is largely self-regulated, and the Attorney Grievance Commission actively investigates complaints from clients and the public in general if at any time the Standards of Conduct for Attorneys are violated. More information concerning standards of professional conduct and procedures for filing a complaint against a lawyer or judge is available at the State Bar of Michigan website, www.michbar.org

Confidentiality and the Attorney-Client Privilege

As discussed above, the relationship between attorney and client is characterized by a high degree of confidentiality. For this reason, anything you tell your lawyer in confidence is protected by the attorney – client privilege, and therefore not subject to disclosure in court. When you meet with your attorney, you may feel inclined to bring a relative or friend with you for guidance or moral support. Do not be offended if your attorney asks this person to leave the room when you are consulting. In some cases, the courts have held that the presence of a third party during communications between an attorney and client can constitute a waiver of the attorney-client privilege. The last thing you want to do is make your conversations with your attorney discoverable and admissible at trial, and presence of a third party during private conversations can do just that. So if you are inclined to bring a friend or relative with you to meetings at your attorney's office or in the courthouse, tell that person to bring a good book and prepare to spend some time in the hallway.

Fee Agreements and Paying for Your Divorce

Be sure to discuss the fee agreement at your first meeting with your attorney. Michigan Rule of Professional Conduct 1.5 governs fee agreements. First and foremost, the fee for legal services must be reasonable. In divorce cases, the fee is nearly always based on an hourly rate. You can get a good idea of the customary hourly rate in your community simply by asking a few lawyers or those who have used their services about their hourly rates. The State Bar of Michigan recently published statistics on attorney billing rates in its 2014 Economics of Law Practice Attorney Income and Billing Rate Summary Report which can be found at www.michbar.org/.../0000151.pdf. This survey breaks down attorney hourly billing rates by county, fields of practice, office location, firm size, and other factors. Depending on the locality, hourly fees vary widely, with lawyers in large metropolitan areas generally charging significantly higher hourly rates than lawyers in rural areas or small towns. While in some cases attorneys do charge flat fees for divorces, the ethical rules prohibit an attorney from collecting a contingent fee in a domestic relations matter. In determining whether a fee is reasonable, the court will look at the experience, reputation and ability of the attorney, the difficulty of the case, the fees customarily charged in similar localities, and other factors. The ethical rules require that the attorney's fee "shall be communicated to the client, preferably in writing, before or within a reasonable time after commencing the representation" (MRPC 1.5(b)). Under no circumstances would I recommend entering into an unwritten fee agreement with your attorney in a domestic case.

At your initial meeting, the attorney should provide a written fee agreement for you to sign. At a minimum, the agreement should contain the following information:

- The scope of the representation. A client may have more than one legal matter pending at the same time when in the middle of a divorce. For example, if you are filing for divorce and also seeking a personal protection order against your soon–to-be ex-spouse because of domestic violence, there are two distinct legal proceedings pending. Be sure you and your attorney clearly agree on the scope of representation. If you expect your attorney to represent you in the personal protection proceeding, the fee agreement must so provide, and the attorney will need to file a separate appearance with the court.
- The hourly rate. Make sure the fee agreement is clear on not only what the attorney will charge, but if paralegals, legal assistants or others will be involved with your matter, what their hourly rate will be.
- Billing increments. The agreement should state whether there is a minimum billing increment, such as one quarter hour or 1/10 hour.
- The amount and terms of the retainer. Most attorneys require a lump sum advance payment before they will file any divorce papers. Attorneys are required to deposit this advance payment into a separate account, usually called an IOLTA (Interest on Lawyer's Trust Account). When deposited in this type of account the money actually belongs to the client until it is earned by the attorney through the rendering of services or incurring of costs, such as filing fees or motion fees. The ethical rules require that retainer fees be refunded to the extent they are unearned, unless the retainer agreement provides to the contrary. Interest on IOLTA accounts is paid by the financial institution directly to the State Bar Foundation, which uses it for law-related charitable purposes.

- Billing frequency. At a minimum, the agreement should provide for monthly invoices which should reflect the amount, if any, remaining in the retainer account.
- The right to liens on marital property. In some cases, if an attorney is owed fees following the conclusion of a divorce case, the attorney will assert a lien against real or personal property in the portion of the marital estate awarded to the client. In order to establish the attorney's right to do this, the fee agreement must so provide.
- The circumstances that allow the attorney to withdraw from representation. An attorney cannot simply quit working for a client in the middle of the case unless the client consents or the court excuses the attorney through a formal order. Reasons an attorney can withdraw may include, by way of example, failure of the client to honor the fee agreement, or a breakdown in the attorney-client relationship.
- The terms of payment expected once the retainer balance is exhausted. The agreement should set forth the attorney's right to request that the retainer account be replenished if this is the expectation. Also, how soon after receiving a bill is the client expected to pay?
- The imposition of interest or late fees on any balance owing beyond the agreed payment period.
- Responsibility for payment of other costs including filing fees, motion fees, photocopies, postage, mileage, transcripts, witness fees, etc.

Do not hesitate to ask your attorney to further explain the fee agreement if it seems vague or incomplete. Some attorneys do not charge for brief phone calls, but others will charge a minimum increment every time they pick up the phone or answer an email. Request that the fee agreement specifically address how these communications will be billed.

You have a right to ask for a ballpark estimate on the total cost of your legal proceeding. However, if your attorney is honest with you, he'll say there is no way to guarantee the total expense, as there are many things an attorney cannot predict. For example, the attorney has no control over the level of conflict between the parties, and if your spouse chooses to file motions and haul you into court every chance he gets, that will significantly increase the cost of your divorce. If an inexperienced or overly aggressive attorney, or one who has an axe to grind with your lawyer, shows up on the other side, this can escalate the expense. In spite of this, most attorneys will attempt to give you a ballpark fee estimate if you ask.

You may be wondering at this early stage how you will ever pay for a divorce, when you are faced with the new economic challenge of splitting one household into two with no corresponding increase in income. If you anticipate difficulty living up to the fee agreement, discuss options for payment with your attorney. Most law offices now accept credit cards, and some practitioners will work on a monthly payment basis with creditworthy clients.

Some additional creative options can be explored early on for payment of fees. Under certain circumstances, the law does provide for payment of all or part of one party's attorney fees by the other party. First, if there is a disparity in ability to pay, the court may order the party with the greater income to pay a fixed amount of the other party's attorney fees. Second, if the court finds that the opposing party's conduct is inappropriately litigious, or for an improper purpose such as to harass, annoy, or cause increased expense to the other party, an award of attorney fees may be included in the final judgment. Some judges will also award a lump sum attorney fee at the beginning of a divorce case if a party files a motion asking for it.

In most divorces, the attorney initiating the action, or sometimes the court of its own initiative, will enter an order prohibiting the parties from liquidating any marital assets without the express consent of the other party. If this is the case, your attorney can negotiate with opposing counsel to make an exception to this order allowing an asset to be liquidated for the purpose of paying attorney fees. This is commonly done with investment accounts, or easily salable assets such as boats, vehicles, guns, etc.

If you or your spouse has a retirement plan such as a 401(k) through an employer, you can explore borrowing from or liquidating one or more of these accounts to pay attorney fees. Discuss with your tax preparer whether an early distribution for this purpose can qualify as a hardship exemption, under which you would not be required to pay the 10% tax penalty.

If you anticipate difficulty paying your legal fees, ask your attorney to explore one of the above options.

Communicating With Your Attorney

Nothing is more vital to the attorney-client relationship than frequent and transparent communication. Here are a few pointers to assist you in effectively communicating with your attorney during your divorce:

- Provide your attorney with up-to-date contact information, including cell phone, landline, home and work telephone numbers, and email address. If you do not check email often, have your attorney note in the file that telephone is your preferred mode of contact.
- When you receive an email from your attorney, always acknowledge it. In the long run, responding by email will save you money, as you do not want to put your attorney in the position of having to follow up emails with telephone calls simply to verify that you received the message.
- Expect to pay for communications. If you are calling your attorney's office in the middle of the day, be aware you are probably pulling him away from another task. If you have signed a fee agreement indicating that the attorney charges for telephone calls, don't call your attorney and ask "Are you going to charge me for this telephone call?" By doing this, you will send the message to the attorney that you do not believe his time or advice are worth anything. This will likely result in a phone call that is shorter than and not as thorough as it should be to discuss the specifics of your case. Most attorneys will not charge for a phone call asking, for instance, "What time do I need to be at the courthouse tomorrow?" But if you are calling to ask more in-depth questions concerning, for example, division of retirement benefits, do not expect the telephone call to be brief, and do not expect it to be free. In fact, your attorney may require that such inquiries take place in person at the office, or at the very least in a prearranged telephone conference

so the attorney can have your file in front of him and be prepared to address the inquiry. It may damage the attorney-client relationship if the attorney starts to feel that you are imposing on her time or continually pumping her for free information when, in the words of Abraham Lincoln, "a lawyer's time and advice are his stock in trade."

- Provide the attorney with as much information in as organized a fashion as possible. The more information your attorney has in the file, the more accurate an analysis you will get regarding likely outcomes. Information gathering is more specifically addressed below.

- If you plan to be away for a vacation, medical procedure, or business travel, let your attorney's office know as early as possible so as to avoid scheduling of court appearances when you are unavailable. If this happens, your attorney will need to file a motion to adjourn or reschedule, resulting in greater expense and inconvenience.

- Use email or written communication often. Most attorneys would prefer to have a letter or email in the file documenting your concerns rather than having to reconstruct things you said during a telephone call when they are attempting to respond to your inquiry. Email, a form of asynchronous communication, can be more effective than a telephone call when an attorney is busy.

- If you want paper copies of all pleadings, correspondence, etc., your attorney should provide them. However, if you are satisfied with electronic copies, let your attorney's office know. In the long run, it should save you money.

- If you disagree with a course of action your attorney is taking, tell her immediately.

- Ask your attorney to prepare a proposed judgment of divorce early on in your case to serve as a template for settlement discussions. If you are familiar with all areas the judgment will ultimately cover, you can begin thinking about a possible settlement.

Information Gathering

As discussed above, the more information you provide your attorney early on, the more effective the representation can be. I recommend, at a minimum, that you provide the following documentation to your lawyer within a few days of signing the retainer agreement:

- If you have been served with divorce papers, copies of everything you received and documentation of the date you were served;
- Full legal names, birth dates, social security numbers for parties and any minor children;
- Any addresses at which the minor children have resided within the past ten years and with whom they lived;
- Health insurance coverage information for the children;
- If you, your spouse or any of your children have ever been involved in any prior court proceeding including divorce, custody, abuse/neglect, guardianship, or domestic violence, provide the year the action was filed and the county.
- Current mortgage statement for any real property owned;
- Itemized budget for the marital home, including mortgage, taxes, utilities, insurance, automobiles, fuel, food, recreation, club memberships, children's activities, school tuition, entertainment, cosmetics, haircuts, pet care, cable and Internet, professional dues, medical, dental and optical, travel, vacation, gifts, clothing, association fees, home maintenance and repairs, vehicle maintenance, debt payments, and any other foreseeable expenditures;
- Current statements for any credit cards showing names of account holders and account numbers;
- Titles to all vehicles, recreational vehicles and watercraft with VINs. If any loans are outstanding, copies of current loan statements;
- Current checking, saving, and investment account statements;

- Retirement account statements (current and from the year you were married if the accounts were premarital) for any IRA, 401(k), 403(b), pension, or retirement annuities;
- Declarations pages from any life insurance policies showing beneficiaries, amount of coverage and, if the policy is a whole life policy, a statement of the cash value and any loan balances;
- Promissory note or any written document evidencing loans from friends or family members;
- Income tax returns and related schedules, w-2s for you and your spouse. If either of you is self-employed, copies of schedule C, K(1) or any corporate returns filed by any business entities in which you or your spouse has an interest;
- Credit reports for you and your spouse. Note: Do not run a credit report on your spouse unless you have authorization to do so. Credit reports can be obtained on line at websites such as www.freeannualcreditreport.com;
- If you have minor children, provide your attorney with a calendar or written schedule of the children's activities, lessons, sports practices, etc. to facilitate an understanding of what might work in scheduling parenting time;
- Police reports for any instances of domestic violence or criminal behavior;
- Blue Book values for all vehicles owned;
- Inventory of personal property. If any item is an heirloom or of extraordinary value (antique, collectible), have it appraised;
- If you or your spouse owns any interest in a corporation, professional practice, partnership or LLC, provide copies of corporate balance sheet or profit/loss statements;
- If you, your spouse or children have any significant health issues or disabilities, provide an explanation of the condition, any treatment anticipated and if the condition interferes with your employment, to what extent and if this has been documented by a physician, copies of medical records to verify;
- Any patents, trademarks or copyrights you or your spouse may own;

- The names and addresses of all healthcare providers for each spouse and the children; if a medical condition is at issue your attorney may ask you to sign an authorization to release medical or counseling records.

The above list is not exhaustive and depending on the issues in your case, your attorney may ask for more documentation. However, if you provide the above documents in an organized format, it will give you and your lawyer a jump start on working toward a resolution.

CHAPTER 3

Divorce Law and Procedure

"There is a higher court than courts of justice and that is
the court of conscience. It supersedes all other courts."
— MAHATMA GANDHI

The Meaning of No-Fault Divorce

Since the early 1970s, Michigan has been a no-fault divorce state, meaning that the parties are not required to plead (state in the complaint or other papers) or prove (show evidence in court) a reason for the divorce, other than the statutory standard which is set forth in every complaint for divorce. The key statutory language provides that a divorce will be granted on proof of the following:

"There has been a breakdown in the marriage relationship to the extent the objects of matrimony have been destroyed and there remains no reasonable likelihood that the marriage can be preserved." (Michigan Compiled Laws Section 552.6)

This is a relatively simple standard to meet, and a judgment of divorce is in nearly all cases granted at what is called the *pro confesso* or *pro con* hearing based upon the plaintiff's testimony that the above standard has been met, without further explanation or presentation of evidence. Understand, however, the no-fault divorce standard does not mean fault is irrelevant in divorce proceedings. In the context of custody and parenting time, the moral fitness of the parties is a key factor. If one party has perpetrated acts of domestic violence against the other, been unfaithful, committed crimes, or abused substances, this conduct can influence custody, parenting time, property settlement and spousal support. Do not let the concept of no-fault divorce stop you from telling your attorney of any of these instances of bad behavior, whether by you or your spouse, as they will most likely be brought up if your case goes to trial. Even in a no-fault divorce jurisdiction the conduct of the parties during the marriage is relevant. The role of fault will be discussed in greater detail in the custody, property division and spousal support discussions below.

Separate Maintenance

Sometimes when clients are ambivalent about filing for divorce they ask me if Michigan recognizes legal separation. The answer is no; but our state does have a procedure known as separate maintenance, which is sometimes utilized in cases where one or both spouses are opposed to divorce on moral or religious grounds. In such an action, the same jurisdictional requirements and standard of proving breakdown of the marriage relationship must be met. A judgment of separate maintenance accomplishes everything a judgment of divorce does, except for dissolution of the marriage. A judgment of separate maintenance divides marital property, addresses child custody, parenting time, child support and spousal support. The only difference is that the people are still married. If the defendant in a separate maintenance action counterclaims for divorce, a judgment of divorce will be granted.

Occasionally, someone will seek a judgment of separate maintenance in an effort to stay "technically married" in order to remain on a spouse's health insurance coverage. I do not recommend this approach, as insurance companies have become wise to the practice and have refined the contractual language in their policies to specifically reference legal separation or separate maintenance as a disqualifying event.

Filing a complaint for divorce can serve as a means of legal separation, as it gives the court jurisdiction to divide responsibilities for paying marital expenses and debt while establishing temporary parenting time, child support and spousal support until the divorce is final.

A judgment of separate maintenance can provide that either party may file a motion to convert the judgment of separate maintenance to one of absolute divorce should either ex-spouse desire to do so.

Jurisdiction, Venue, and Other Preliminary Matters

Jurisdiction means that a court has authority or power to make a legal decision. Two types of jurisdiction are important in divorce. First, the complaint for divorce must establish that the court has jurisdiction to grant a divorce to the one asking for it. In Michigan a court cannot grant a divorce unless, immediately prior to filing the complaint for divorce, either the plaintiff (the person filing the complaint for divorce) or the defendant (the person responding to the complaint for divorce) has been a resident of the state of Michigan for at least 180 days. In addition, for a court of a particular county to have jurisdiction over a divorce proceeding, one or both spouses must have been a resident of that county for at least 10 days immediately prior to filing the complaint for divorce (Michigan Compiled Laws section 552.9).

Once a court starts a divorce case, that court in nearly all cases must adjudicate the divorce to conclusion, even if the plaintiff moves out of the county, unless one of the parties files a motion to change venue (location of the proceeding). If one party still resides in the county that has jurisdiction or in a contiguous county, the court will not change venue to a different county. So if you plan to move, discuss this with your attorney. This is of greatest concern if there are minor children involved, as the court that grants your divorce will continue to exercise jurisdiction over the children and will have exclusive power to determine parenting time, support, custody, and other important aspects of the children's care for years to come after the divorce is granted. In certain cases it is preferable to wait to file the complaint for divorce until after the move, as it is more convenient to have the action decided in the new county of residence.

The second type of jurisdiction is personal jurisdiction, or the authority of the court to make decisions affecting a particular person. To be subject to personal jurisdiction, the defendant in a divorce case must be served with the summons and complaint. In most cases, this is not difficult, especially where the parties reside in the same locale. However, where the defendant's whereabouts are unknown or if he is in a different city, state, or even out of the country, it may be more challenging to establish personal jurisdiction. If you anticipate problems locating your spouse to serve papers on him or her, let your attorney know, as this can add time and expense. Even in the most challenging geographical circumstances, the court rules provide for alternate service by publication and other means.

Michigan law also requires a waiting period before a judgment of divorce can be entered. This begins to run on the date the summons is issued by the court, regardless of the date the complaint is actually served on the defendant. In divorces with children, the minimum waiting period is 182 days. Where no minor children are involved, this is shortened to 60 days. In certain cases, where good cause is shown, the court will shorten the waiting period. However, this is unusual, and do not expect the waiting period to be shortened absent some compelling circumstance. Talk to your attorney about a reasonable timeline. In many counties, it takes longer than the statutory minimum for a judgment of divorce to enter, especially if issues such as custody are contested.

The Basic Paperwork

The person who initiates the complaint for divorce is called the plaintiff. The other spouse is the defendant. A divorce proceeding is commenced when the plaintiff files a summons and complaint. The summons is a form filed by the plaintiff's attorney telling the other party that a divorce action has been filed. The summons advises the defendant that he or she has 21 days to file an answer if served personally, and 28 days if served by certified mail or other means. The complaint is a relatively brief document which in most cases simply sets forth the jurisdictional requirements for divorce and requests that the marriage be dissolved and property and debts be divided. In most cases, the complaint for divorce does not contain specific requests, other than for fair and equitable division of the property and a determination of custody and support if minor children are involved.

If you are served with divorce papers, immediately give your attorney copies of everything you receive. Make careful note of the date you were served and provide that information to the attorney's office. If you receive anything by mail, keep the envelope, as the postmark may serve as evidence of when the items were mailed. If you do not respond to a complaint for divorce, you can be defaulted. No matter what your spouse has said to you, be sure to have your attorney file an answer to preserve your legal right to contest the divorce, even if you believe you will work everything out. I have been in court countless times when a defendant, having been defaulted, has tried to convince the judge that the default should be set aside based on assurances from the plaintiff spouse that everything would be worked out amicably, thus the defendant does not worry about filing an answer. Much to the defendant's surprise, when the matter is not resolved through nego-tiations, the plaintiff files a default. This is not a good place to be, and a de-fault can be avoided simply by filing an answer to the complaint for divorce, a relatively simple task. If you have been served with a notice of default for failing to answer the complaint for divorce, let your attorney know immedi-ately. In certain cases, a default can be set aside. Even if a default is not set aside, the person in default still has the right to appear at a hearing before the judgment of divorce is entered, where the judge must make a finding that the judgment is fair and equitable and in the best interest of the minor children before signing the judgment.

People often ask whether a pending complaint for divorce can be set aside if the parties reconcile. The answer is yes; however, if the defendant has filed an answer, the court will not dismiss the divorce unless both parties sign the stipulation for dismissal. If the plaintiff files a complaint for divorce and the defendant agrees that divorce is inevitable, sometimes the defendant will file a counterclaim, making it known that the defendant is also asking for a divorce, and even if the plaintiff has a change of heart, the defendant can push the process through to conclusion. Be sure to discuss with your attorney whether it would be advisable to file a counterclaim if you are the defendant.

The plaintiff in a divorce case is also required to file a verified statement which provides basic information on the parties and their children, as well as a record of divorce to be placed on file with the Office of Vital Records in Lansing once the divorce is finalized. The filing fee for a new divorce case is $150. In cases with children, there is also a judgment fee of $80 which must be paid when the divorce is finalized.

Ex Parte Motions and Temporary Orders

The marriage relationship is one of mutual trust and respect. When a new divorce case is filed, whether anticipated or not, the relationship between spouses is turned on its head. Trust breaks down, secrets may be exposed, and the playing field is drastically changed. For this reason, your attorney may file *ex parte* motions for relief on an emergency basis at the time the complaint for divorce is filed. An *ex parte* motion is one decided by the judge without requiring the parties to attend a hearing. For *ex parte* relief to be granted, the moving party must show, through a sworn affidavit, that if the relief requested is not granted, irreparable harm will likely result. Most commonly, these motions are necessary when minor children are involved, or when one party is concerned that the other will liquidate or conceal marital assets, depriving the other of access to funds necessary to carry on until the divorce judgment is finalized. Another commonly utilized *ex parte* motion is one for exclusive possession of the marital home. Each of these will be discussed below.

Where minor children are involved, the parties have likely been residing together and sharing parental responsibilities and time with the children. However, when a complaint for divorce is filed, one party often leaves the marital home. A party's absence does not deprive that parent of the right to spend time with the children. Even after the complaint for divorce is filed, both parents in reality have equal rights to spend time with the children, and to make important decisions regarding the children's day-to-day care and upbringing. In order to avoid a chaotic situation where the parents are battling for power and control of the children, the plaintiff's attorney may file a motion for *ex parte* relief asking for temporary custody. Typically, this is done when the spouse filing for divorce fears that the other spouse may remove the children from the marital home, take them out of state, abuse them, or deprive the other spouse of access to the children. This often presents an extremely volatile situation which must be handled with skill and compassion. If a temporary custody order is entered *ex parte*, it will clearly define the rights of both parents, and may even set a temporary parenting time schedule for the noncustodial parent. These temporary custody orders, while helpful in avoiding a chaotic situation where parents are jockeying for control over the children, are usually short-lived, as most courts now utilize a procedure for coordination conferences, where more comprehensive temporary custody and parenting time orders are entered. Coordination conferences are discussed below.

Another commonly utilized *ex parte* order is one preserving marital assets. Because these orders are almost always binding on both parties to the divorce and are intended to preserve the *status quo*, they are routinely granted. A motion seeking this type of order must be verified by affidavit. These orders are commonly sought when one of the parties owns liquid assets that could be easily concealed or dissipated, such as bank accounts, mutual funds, antiques, collectibles, or other readily salable items. If one of the parties is self-employed or has an ownership interest in a business, the other party can seek an *ex parte* order requiring that business assets also be frozen until a clear accounting of all assets is provided. The intent of these orders is not to deprive either party of the right to access funds as required in the ordinary course of business, but to prevent either party from dissipating marital assets in an effort to deprive the other of access, both on a temporary basis and as a final distribution in the judgment of divorce.

A third type of order, often sought in conjunction with an order of temporary custody of the minor children, is for exclusive possession of the marital home. In the great majority of cases, married couples hold real estate jointly as husband and wife, affording both equal rights to occupy the marital home while the divorce is pending. In certain cases, due to the level of stress and anxiety associated with a newly filed divorce, one spouse finds it necessary to bar the other from residing in the home. This type of relief is commonly sought in cases of domestic violence (See chapter 9). In less extreme cases, some judges will grant these motions on a mere showing that there has been arguing or verbal abuse in the presence of the children, resulting in emotional distress.

All *ex parte* orders are subject to a statutory objection period. For an order to be effective, it must be served on the other party, just as is done with the summons and complaint. All *ex parte* orders must state that the party served with the order may file an objection within 14 days, and that a hearing on the order will be held within 21 days or the order will become a temporary order. If you are served with any kind of *ex parte* or temporary order, provide a copy of it to your attorney immediately and discuss whether it would be advisable to file an objection.

Discovery

In many divorces, particularly those with significant financial assets or where custody is in dispute, the attorneys will conduct discovery, which is a legitimate part of the legal process designed to gather the facts needed for settlement or trial. While it is the client's duty to provide financial and personal information to the attorney so she can better assess the possible outcome of the case, negotiate a fair resolution or prepare for trial, there may be information that you simply do not have at your disposal. Many times both spouses have a reasonable grasp of their overall financial picture. However, in cases where one spouse is clueless as to finances, it is vital that the attorney for that party conduct thorough discovery to obtain an accurate picture of the financial condition of both. For example, you need to know if your spouse has credit cards on which you are jointly obligated. You also need to know how much your spouse has in her retirement accounts, and whether she has any bank accounts unknown to you. Where parties have anticipated divorce, they may scramble to transfer assets into someone else's name; they may open savings or investment accounts in other towns or even out of the country, or sell assets to save up for legal fees. All these activities are relevant when it comes to assessing the marital estate and a possible divorce settlement. One of the most common areas for attorney malpractice is failure to conduct adequate asset discovery, so you can anticipate that unless you have virtually no assets, your attorney will want to do some formal discovery.

Interrogatories and requests for production of documents are two widely utilized discovery methods in divorce cases. Answering written discovery can be a tedious and unpleasant task, as the inquiries are often lengthy and redundant, causing the recipient to feel that they serve no purpose other than to harass and drive up the legal fees. However, the court rules authorize written discovery in divorce cases, and it is commonplace. If the questioning is excessive, redundant or completely irrelevant to the issues at hand, your attorney may file a motion for protective order.

If your attorney asks you to answer interrogatories, it is your job to provide the information. If your attorney believes the requests are improper, he can file an objection and ask the court to strike the discovery requests. However, whether answers to the requests are ultimately served on opposing counsel or not, your attorney will probably expect to have all of the information in his file. The court rules provide that interrogatories and requests for production of documents are to be answered under oath within 28 days after they are served on the responding party. Keep in mind that your answers to written discovery constitute testimony, as they are in the form of a sworn statement. Anything you say in those answers can be used at trial, and if you withhold any material facts, the opposing attorney will do his best to make you out to be a liar. So tell the truth and provide complete responses.

Another means of discovery, less common than the written variety, is the deposition. This is an opportunity for the attorneys to orally question the parties or any witness under oath before a court reporter prior to trial. This is often done in highly contested custody cases in an effort to understand the opposing party's position, to evaluate how the person will perform as a witness at trial, and gather facts to prepare. Depositions are also a common discovery practice in high net worth divorces or cases where the parties are self-employed and income is difficult to determine. In more complex cases, the attorneys may conduct depositions of counselors or medical professionals, accountants, business valuation specialists and anyone else who may testify as a witness at the trial. If you are required to give a deposition, be sure to meet with your attorney well in advance to prepare.

Your medical, psychological and counseling records may be subpoenaed. However, before any of your medical providers or any counseling professional may disclose any of your health information, they must obtain written authorization from you. If one of your healthcare providers or counselors tells you they have received a subpoena or other request from your spouse's attorney, let your attorney know immediately. In custody cases, psychological and counseling records are often highly relevant. Your involvement in a divorce or custody case does not mean you no longer have a right to privacy, though. If you choose to assert the physician-patient or therapist-client privileges, this can protect you from having to disclose your medical or counseling records. However, one consequence to exercising these privileges is that the court may prohibit the person exercising them from introducing any of his or her own medical or psychological evidence. If you anticipate that your medical or counseling records will be subpoenaed, let your attorney know early in the proceeding so you can formulate a strategy for responding.

Finally, be forewarned that all your banking records, telephone bills, employment records, social media accounts, and essentially every aspect of your personal life may be the subject of subpoena as you move through the divorce process.

Friend of the Court Coordination Conferences

The Friend of the Court is an extension of the Family Division of the Circuit Court whose role is to provide assistance to the court and furnish the court with recommendations related to matters such as custody, parenting time, and child support. The Friend of the Court is also responsible for enforcement of and assisting in the collection of child support and spousal support.

Most Michigan counties now utilize the Friend of the Court coordination conference early in divorces with minor children. This may also be referred to as a conciliation conference, or early Friend of the Court mediation. The meeting is intended to encourage the parties to begin productively discussing custody, parenting time and support and to define the rights of each parent. This may include recommending a temporary order for legal and physical custody and child support. The Friend of the Court seldom gets involved in temporary spousal support issues or possession of the marital home.

In most counties, the plaintiff and defendant will receive a letter from the Friend of the Court worker assigned to their case shortly after the complaint for divorce has been filed. This letter will provide a date and time for the Friend of the Court coordination conference, usually within a few weeks following the initiation of the new divorce case. Most counties will allow attorneys to attend the conference, but for the most part they are not allowed to actively participate. The parties are required to appear and confer with the worker concerning the children's needs and are encouraged to agree upon a custody and parenting time plan. Where the parents do not agree, the Friend of the Court worker will prepare a written recommendation and order based upon information gathered in the coordination conference and submit it to the judge and to the parties by mail, with notice of the right to object and the procedure for doing so.

If neither party objects to this recommendation within 21 days, it becomes a temporary court order that will remain in place until otherwise modified. The parties are also required to produce income information at the meeting, and the Friend of the Court worker will calculate child support based upon income information provided and the number of overnights assigned to each parent. The support calculations are also subject to objection by either party. If either party objects to the custody, parenting time or support provisions contained in the recommended order, the court will schedule the objection for a hearing before the judge. At the hearing, the judge will either adopt the recommendation of the Friend of the Court and enter it as an order, modify the recommendation, or schedule an evidentiary hearing if factual disputes exist.

The coordination conference can prove invaluable in bringing some sanity to the often chaotic weeks following the filing of a complaint for divorce. It should be taken seriously, as it presents an opportunity to resolve important issues that affect the children.

Name Change

If you or your spouse changed your name on marriage, either of you has the right to change your name back to a previous one. If you are unsure whether you want to change your name, give this careful consideration, as it is much easier to do so in conjunction with a divorce than through a separate legal process, which requires payment of a fee, publication, fingerprinting and a hearing. A divorcing spouse is not limited to a previous name, but in fact may change his or her name to anything, provided the change is not for an improper or unlawful purpose. Prior to entry of judgment, be sure to review the judgment and make sure any name change you desire is included. Following entry of the judgment, you will need to report the change to the Michigan Secretary of State, the Office of Social Security, and your employer.

Same-Sex Marriage

On June 26, 2015, in the landmark decision of *Obergefell v. Hodges,* Nos 14-556, 140562, 14-571 and 14-574, the U.S. Supreme Court struck down Michigan's 2004 law limiting marriage to heterosexual couples, as well as restrictions against same-sex marriages in all 50 states. Now all states must recognize same-sex marriages, even where a marriage was solemnized in another state where it was legal at a time when it was not recognized in Michigan. Many Michigan statutes, court rules and forms are being revised in light of this ruling.

Prior to *Obergefell,* same-sex couples who had legally married in other states and then came to Michigan were without a forum in this state to address a divorce, as Michigan did not recognize their marriages. While *Obergefell* settles the issue of validity of the marriage, the law remains unclear as to what date such marriages actually begin for purposes of divorce. Thus, determining property rights of same-sex spouses will be challenging for the courts until this area of the law is settled.

Reconciliation

As discussed above, a divorce is not final until the judge has signed the judgment of divorce, and there is a built- in mandatory waiting period between the filing of the complaint and entry of judgment in all divorces. One reason for the delay is to allow the parties to fully explore reconciliation before finalizing a judgment of divorce. Approximately 20% of the divorce cases I file do not result in a final judgment of divorce. Sometimes, when people separate and begin to experience life without their spouse, the financial realities of child support, and other impacts of divorce, they reconsider their decision and decide to give the marriage another chance. When this occurs, one of two things may happen. In some counties, the judges are open to placing the matter on "administrative closing," sometimes for two or three months to extend the waiting period and to give the parties a chance to attend counseling and explore whether the marriage can be restored.

In the alternative, the parties may decide to stipulate to complete dismissal of the complaint for divorce. If this is done, in the event the marriage does not work out, a new complaint for divorce must be filed, another filing fee must be paid, and everything starts over again.

If you are considering reconciliation, ask your attorney whether you might be able to delay the matter for a few months to allow time to fully explore whether your marriage can be saved.

CHAPTER 4

Child Custody and Parenting Time

> "When Mom and Dad went to war the only
> prisoners they took were the children."
> — Pat Conroy

Basic Custody Law and Terminology

Every judgment of divorce must award legal and physical custody of the minor children to one or both parents or, in extremely rare cases, to a third party. Do all you can to better understand the concepts of legal and physical custody early in the proceedings so you will be able to discuss custody intelligently with your attorney. If custody will be disputed, you and your attorney need to take certain precautions, and you must prepare yourself for what is potentially an emotionally draining and lengthy process.

The paramount consideration in a custody determination is the best interests of the child. The law does not require that time spent with the children be divided equally between the parents, even with joint custody. Consideration of the children's rights must come before any inquiry regarding the rights of the parents. Remember: Children are not property, and they are not divided, equally or otherwise. If you review the Michigan Child Custody Act and the custody factors discussed below, you will note that none of the factors considers the rights of the parents.

It is important to first understand the difference between legal and physical custody. Legal custody is defined as when a parent has the responsibility and right to make major decisions regarding the child's upbringing (such as medical treatment, what school the child will attend, religious instruction, and participation in extracurricular activities). If the judge believes the parents cannot communicate effectively and cooperatively to work together for the benefit of their child, sole legal custody will be awarded to one parent. However, if the parents demonstrate ability and willingness to work together in making important decisions, most judges are inclined to favor joint legal custody.

Physical custody refers to the right of the parents to have the child physically present with them. The parent with physical custody is responsible for routine matters regarding the child's day-to-day activities and general welfare when the child is present. Like legal custody, physical custody can be either joint or sole. If one parent has sole physical custody, the other parent will have parenting time, which is sometimes referred to as visitation. Even if one party has sole physical custody, each parent has the authority to make routine decisions during their own parenting time.

At the request of either parent, the court must consider an order of joint custody. If the parents agree on joint custody, the court must order it unless the court determines by clear and convincing evidence that joint custody is not in the best interest of the child. When deciding, the judge must state on the record the reasons for granting or denying the request. A judge may consider joint custody without a parent's request. In addition to the normal factors considered when deciding custody, with joint custody judges must also consider whether the parents will be able to cooperate and generally agree concerning important decisions affecting the welfare of the child.

It is presumed to be in a child's best interest to have a close relationship with both parents. In making a custody determination, a judge should attempt to award custody in a manner that will promote a strong relationship between children and their parents.

While it is preferable to arrive at a custody agreement through negotiation or mediation, in cases where the parties disagree on custody, the court must make the determination. This can be a very complex inquiry. In most counties, the court utilizes the Friend of the Court to perform custody evaluations and make a recommendation to the court in contested custody cases.

Custody Evaluation and Investigation

If you anticipate that you and your spouse will be unable to agree on custody, ask your attorney about filing a motion for custody assessment. If the court grants this motion, it will assign your case to a custody investigator, usually an employee of the Friend of the Court, or in some counties an independent contractor. The Child Custody Act also authorizes the court to utilize a guardian ad litem, often an attorney appointed by the court to investigate and submit a report regarding the child's best interests. The judge can also appoint a lawyer-guardian ad litem for the children if it appears the children's interests are not being adequately represented. The lawyer-guardian ad litem can file motions and call witnesses on behalf of the children. Custody investigators are often psychologists or social workers who specialize in investigating and determining which parent in a contested custody case is more capable of providing care for the child consistent with the child's best interest. If your case is assigned to an investigator, he or she may visit your home, and you and your spouse will be interviewed extensively regarding the details of both parents' relationships with the children. Be prepared to answer questions concerning such details as:

- Who bathes, dresses, or grooms the child?
- How is discipline administered?
- Which parent usually attends parent-teacher conferences and school events?
- Which parent helps the child with homework?
- Does the family have a religious tradition? Is religion discussed in the home and by which parent? Do the parents pray or read scriptures with the children? Do the parents take the children to church? How long has the child attended this particular church?

- If the child is afraid of something, which parent is more likely to offer comfort?
- Have the parents taught the child about human sexuality, and, if so, what was the role of each parent in doing that?
- Who cooks and prepares meals for the child?
- Which parent more often takes the child to school?
- Who buys clothing for the child?
- Does the child have any responsibilities around the house? How are family household chores divided?
- Does the child have any pets?
- What leisure activities do the parents participate in with the child? Does either parent coach a sport? Which parent attends sporting events?
- Has either parent ever abused the child, physically, sexually or emotionally?
- What are the sleeping arrangements in the home? Do the children share a bedroom or a bed with anyone else? Does the child ever sleep with one or both parents?
- Do the parents use alcohol or drugs, and are they involved in pornography, gambling or other addictive behaviors? Does either parent smoke? If so, is it in the presence of the child or in the house or vehicle?
- Does either parent use inappropriate, foul or obscene language in the presence of the child?
- What are the child's favorite toys, television shows, songs, books, computer games?
- Is one parent more likely than the other to utilize safety precautions such as a car seat or bicycle helmet?
- Describe your parenting styles and those of the other parent. What are your strengths and weaknesses as a parent?
- What is your work schedule? Who cares for the child when you are working? Are you required to work overtime or be on call? Do you travel for work?

- Is one parent more able to provide for the basic needs of the child, including clothing, food, shelter, and medical care?
- Does either party have a significant other? Has this person been introduced to the child, and, if so, how would you characterize the relationship?
- Does the child enjoy relationships with siblings, aunts and uncles, grandparents, or other relatives?
- What kinds of things do you do to facilitate a close relationship between the child and the other parent?
- Does either parent have health concerns that might affect his or her ability to parent the child?

The investigator may interview the children and other individuals familiar with your family, including teachers, counselors, daycare providers, friends, neighbors and relatives, and examine medical and school records, social service and child protective services reports, if any.

Once the investigation is complete, the Friend of the Court office will provide a comprehensive report and recommendation to the court and attorneys. While the investigative report is not in and of itself determinative of custody, it is an important piece of evidence the judge must consider. If there is a custody trial, your attorney will most likely subpoena the investigator, who may testify concerning the opinions contained in the report. The Child Custody Act provides that information contained in a Friend of the Court custody investigation report is admissible as evidence under most circumstances.

Michigan's Child Custody Factors and the Best Interests of the Child

The custody investigation, and the ultimate custody determination, are based upon the following "best interests of the child" factors in the Child Custody Act:

(a) The love, affection, and other emotional ties existing between the parties involved and the child.

(b) The capacity and disposition of the parties involved to give the child love, affection, and guidance and the continuation of the education and raising of the child in his or her religion or creed, if any.

(c) The capacity and disposition of the parties involved to provide the child with food, clothing, medical care, or other remedial care recognized and permitted under the laws of this state in place of medical care, and other material needs.

(d) The length of time the child has lived in a stable, satisfactory environment, and the desirability of maintaining continuity.

(e) The permanence, as a family unit, of the existing or proposed custodial home or homes.

(f) The moral fitness of the parties involved.

(g) The mental and physical health of the parties involved.

(h) The home, school, and community record of the child.

(i) The reasonable preference of the child, if the court considers the child to be of sufficient age to express preference.

(j) The willingness and ability of each of the parties to facilitate and encourage a close and continuing parent-child relationship between the child and the other parent or the child and the parents.

(k) Domestic violence, regardless of whether the violence was directed at or witnessed by the child.

(l) Any other factor considered by the court to be of relevance to a particular child custody dispute. (Michigan Compiled Laws sec. 722.23)

At a custody hearing, the judge must listen to testimony of the parties and any witnesses and make findings on the record with respect to each factor, stating whether the parents are equal, or if one or the other prevails. While each factor is important, no single factor is given greater weight than the others, nor does the fact that one parent prevails on more factors than the other necessarily determine the ultimate decision.

Preparing for the Custody Trial

Before deciding custody, the court is required to examine the relationships of both parents with the child using the above factors. Because divorces with children require at a minimum six months from filing of complaint to entry of final judgment, there is typically an extended period of time where the parties are subject to a temporary custody order pending a final determination of custody and parenting time. This can serve as a trial run, affording the parents and the child an opportunity to adjust to the new living arrangements and their evolving relationships. In addition, it provides an opportunity for the court to observe the parties interacting with one another and the child, to gauge the level of conflict between the parents, and to allow the parents to develop a track record of separate parenting on which a final custody determination can be based.

In the early stages of divorce, you may believe that custody will be easily resolved. Regardless, you must behave as though you are being observed by the custody investigator at all times. The way to win a custody case is not to think about the custody case, but to concentrate wholeheartedly on what is in the best interest of your children. By doing so you are in fact preparing for a custody trial and putting yourself in the best position to achieve a favorable outcome. For this reason, I have developed the following list of essential principles.

Ten Essential Principles for Parents in Custody Cases

1. **Obey all court orders regarding custody, parenting time, and support.** The Friend of the Court and the judge in your case will likely expend great effort to come up with a custody and parenting time arrangement that is in your child's best interest. If you do not abide by the court's orders, it will increase conflict in your case, cause emotional upset to the child and the other parent, and will ultimately land you back in court. If you simply cannot live with an order of the court, talk to your attorney about the procedure for filing a motion to change

the order. Do not take it upon yourself to decide which orders are worthy of your obedience. Disobeying a court's order is a surefire way of getting on the judge's bad side and setting yourself up for failure in a custody case.

2. **Never say anything negative about the other parent in the presence of the children.**

Michigan law requires that the following statement be included in all judgments of divorce with minor children:

> The minor children shall have the inherent right to the natural affection and love of both parents, and neither parent shall do anything to estrange, discredit, diminish or cause disrespect for the natural affections of the children for the other parent.

The "inherent rights clause" is an important factor in custody determinations. This protects the child's right to a close relationship with both parents. This is an area where parents commonly slip up during the pendency of a divorce. Even in the most amicable divorces, the parents inevitably harbor some degree of resentment or anger toward one another, which, if they are not extremely careful, may spill over in the presence of the children. A simple roll of the eyes when the other parent's name is mentioned, probing questions to the child after parenting time regarding the other parent's behaviors or careless conversations about the other parent with third parties overheard by the children can cause irreparable damage and negatively impact your custody case.

3. **Do not be overly legalistic or demanding in your expectations of the other parent. Instead, offer a measure of flexibility and grace. You and the children will benefit.**

You would be amazed how difficult this one is for some people. I have actually had a client call me to ask "If she is five minutes late for parenting time, can I call the police?" I hope you get the clue from the caption that the answer is a resounding no. In fact, do not involve the police in parenting time concerns unless someone's health or safety is in immediate jeopardy. The mere presence of a police cruiser at a parenting time exchange causes great emotional trauma for children, especially the very young. I am continually amazed at how many people find it necessary to summon law enforcement, creating a dramatic crime scene whenever parenting time does not quite go as planned. A good rule of thumb is that if you expect any leniency from your ex, you must show leniency. While it seems elementary, in my experience many people do not understand this basic principle. If you take it to heart, your children will benefit, and you will quickly win the judge's favor.

4. **Minimize your use of social media and text messaging.**

While social media can be a useful tool in communicating and maintaining relationships, I encourage my clients to greatly decrease or even eliminate their activities on sites such as Facebook, Twitter, Instagram and other social media. If you are under the microscope of your soon-to-be ex-spouse and her attorney, as well as a custody investigator, you do not need acquaintances posting pictures of you at your friend's bachelor party, at the beach, or with your new flame. In most cases, you have no control over what others will post about you. And don't use Facebook or other social media to send important messages about parenting time to your children or your soon-to-be ex-spouse. This is simply asking for trouble. I encourage my clients to communicate using telephone calls or email, rather than text messages. In my opinion, texting is simply too quick and informal, is done on the fly, and is often misconstrued or sent off in haste or emotion. If your communication is by email your messages are likely more well thought out and logical than those dictated on the go from behind the wheel (don't even think of trying this) or in the line at the supermarket.

5. **Keep a detailed diary of all parent-child interactions.**

In a custody case, expect detailed inquiries regarding, for example, how often you and the other parent attend parent-teacher conferences, church, sporting events, or medical appointments. You will be asked how often you work through the dinner hour or out of town. You may remember several occasions over the past year when your spouse stayed out into the wee hours of the night drinking and was unable to pull himself out of bed the next day to get the children off to school. These tidbits are all part of a custody case and because of their importance should be noted in a journal. Otherwise, if you cannot remember the dates, times, and places, you can be greatly discredited on cross-examination. You can testify with greater credibility if you have some type of record to back it up.

6. **Remember that your soon-to-be ex can try to turn molehills into mountains during a custody case.**

I tell my clients that during a custody case a person who drinks one beer per month may suddenly be called an alcoholic by the other party. The parent who owns a gun collection may be called a weapon fanatic; the occasional buyer of lottery tickets may be portrayed as a gambling addict. It is difficult to refute these allegations if they come unexpectedly. I remind people involved in a custody dispute that their behavior must be above reproach, and that perceptions can be misleading.

7. **If you have a relationship with a new significant other, do not introduce the children to that person until after the divorce is final.**

While the courts recognize that a person has a right to move on after a divorce, the fact of the matter is you are still married until the divorce is final. The rule of law in custody cases is stability. One of the custody factors is the permanence and stability of the family unit. If you are perceived as ready to bring dramatic change to your family unit before your divorce is final, this can harm your custody case. Some judges may go so far as to enter a temporary order prohibiting the parties from having third-party romantic interests present during parenting time. The six-month cooling off period in divorces with children allows time for the children to adjust to the new family structure. Most judges do not approve of a parent introducing a new significant other into the mix when the children have not been given a chance to adjust. Judges tend to see this as unnecessarily ramping up conflict and emotion, as well as creating undue confusion for the children.

8. **Take full advantage of parenting time and do not rely on others to fulfill your parenting responsibilities.**

   It can greatly damage a custody case when an attorney stands up and vigorously argues that his client needs more time with the children, only to be faced with evidence that his client did not exercise what parenting time he already had, or that the client frequently left the children in the care of another to engage in other pursuits. I recall one client who vigorously argued for increased parenting time, only to have opposing counsel produce a record showing that he failed to show up 40% of the time, and when he did show up, he regularly allowed his new girlfriend to watch the children for hours on end while he went off fishing or hunting with his buddies. This guy came off as truly insincere, and his wife's argument that he was trying to get more parenting time only as a means of decreasing his child support quickly caught the judge's attention.

9. **Recognize differences in parenting styles and philosophies.**

   The court understands that no two people parent exactly alike. Do your best to display an understanding of this as you move through a custody case. Judges perceive parents who are overly critical or picky of the other parent's interactions with the child as tending to alienate the child from the other parent, and as unwilling to facilitate a close relationship. You may be a gourmet cook, and your spouse may feed the kids corndogs and chicken nuggets every night. He may be a marathon runner and believe that the children need to exercise daily, while you may be a couch potato satisfied to do nothing more than watch television and read when you have the children. You may be deeply religious, spending time studying the Scriptures daily, and he may have no interest in spiritual things. There is a wide range of what is considered acceptable parenting by the judges, and they have seen most everything on the spectrum. You will make more headway in your custody case if you focus on the big picture. Custody cases are generally not won or lost on the kinds of foods parents serve, what they watch on TV, or how they spend their time in general. Unless a parent's conduct can be deemed abusive or neglectful, the courts recognize great variance and discretion in parenting styles, and so should you.

10. **Remember that even after the marriage ends, you and your ex will still be parenting partners.**

Your relationship with your soon–to-be ex-spouse is changing dramatically. You are no longer lovers and most likely not even friends. However, like it or not, you are business partners in the most important sense. You are jointly responsible for the well-being of the children you brought into the world together. You must continue to work together with your child's best interest at heart, regardless of how you feel about one another. If you hurt one another, you are hurting your children. It may help to look at this as a business partnership. This will get easier as time goes by. If you are struggling with this, I strongly recommend that you seek professional advice, preferably co-parenting counseling. In high conflict cases, judges will sometimes order this. Ideally, you and your spouse would agree to attend voluntarily, setting an excellent example for the children.

Many of our courts offer a variety of resources to divorced parents on co-parenting. Check with your county office of the Friend of the Court to see what resources are available locally.

Parenting Time

Parenting time, referred to by some as visitation, plays an important role in maintaining the parent-child relationship after divorce. Every judgment of divorce must contain parenting time provisions. In most cases, parenting time is set forth in some detail in the judgment of divorce. However, in cases where the parents have shown an ability to communicate and work together cooperatively, a parenting time order may be quite general, stating, for example, "Parenting time with the minor children shall be as agreed upon between the parties" or "Defendant shall have regular and frequent parenting time with the minor children at such times as the parties shall agree." The custody and parenting time statute provides that a court shall enter an order of specific parenting time if a parent requests it.

At the other end of the spectrum, often in high conflict cases, the parenting time order may be extremely detailed, setting forth the exact time and place of parenting exchanges, who will provide transportation, whether third parties may or may not be present at parenting time, etc. In setting parenting time, the court will consider all of the above "best interests of the child" factors.

Many counties publish parenting time policies as guidelines for parents. These policies as a rule gradually increase parenting time for the non-custodial parent based on the ages of the children. They also provide guidance in dividing holidays. No two parenting time cases are the same, as families differ widely in their work schedules and how they spend their leisure time. Where parties geographically separate after divorce, distance considerations may provide additional challenges.

Discuss parenting time with your attorney in the early stages of your divorce. If you anticipate moving, even within your county, this can greatly impact parenting time, especially if you will be locating to a different school district. Michigan law requires that any time a parent moves to a location more than 100 miles from the original home of the children, that parent must seek the court's approval. Even in cases where the move is closer than 100 miles, if it effectively disrupts either parent's custodial environment or renders the parenting time plan unworkable, it will be necessary to ask the court to modify the custody and parenting time orders.

The Michigan Friend of the Court Bureau publishes a Model Parenting Time Guideline which, while not adopted by all counties, serves as a guideline for counties to develop their own policies and procedures. The Model Guideline and parenting time policies of most Michigan counties are published on the Michigan Courts website: www.courts.mi.gov/administration/scao/officesprogram.

In addition to the best interest factors discussed above, the court will look at practical considerations in arriving at a parenting time plan. The parents' work schedules, the children's extracurricular activities and school schedules, special needs, transportation issues, and a host of other factors come into play when arriving at a workable parenting time schedule.

Parents going through divorce commonly state that their goal is to obtain precisely equal parenting time between the parents. While this sometimes works, in many cases it is simply unrealistic. In situations where, for example, one parent has been a full-time stay-at-home caregiver for the children and the other parent has devoted a great deal of energy and time to a demanding career, the court may order a traditional parenting time arrangement, with the established stay-at-home parent having primary custody and parenting time during the week, and the other parent having parenting time on alternating weekends. In the interest of stability, a judge may hesitate to change an arrangement that has worked economically and kept the children healthy and happy during the marriage just so the parents can feel they have equal rights to time with the children. Realistically, children do not spend exactly 50% of their time with each parent during a marriage, so there is no requirement that time be spent equally after the marriage has ended.

Supervised Parenting Time

In some cases, the court orders that parenting time be supervised by a third party. Courts sometimes order supervision of one or both parents when there has been abuse, neglect, or domestic violence in the household. The court may also order supervision of parenting time when a parent voices a rational fear, based on the other parent's statements or behaviors, that the parent may kidnap the child and flee the jurisdiction of the court, or if the parent has a tendency to badmouth the other parent in an effort to alienate the children.

Supervised parenting time is normally ordered in only the most extreme cases. Typically, a supervisor can be anyone appointed by the court or by agreement. Where one of the parties has been accused of abuse or neglect, the court may order supervised therapeutic parenting time with a professional counselor, social worker or psychologist. While potentially effective, professional supervision often presents practical challenges with scheduling and can be quite expensive. Some counties have agencies that provide professional parenting time supervision by trained personnel, usually for less than a licensed counselor charges. While supervision may be necessary in many cases, it does have significant drawbacks. It often takes place by necessity at uncomfortable or unfamiliar environments like the mall or a restaurant play area. While the children may enjoy this for a time, it is highly preferable to have parenting time in a familiar and private place such as the home of a parent or grandparent. While the children's safety is important, the ultimate goal should be to transition out of supervised parenting time and foster a relationship of trust between the parents. In some cases, the court may structure an incremental increase in unsupervised parenting time to facilitate the transition.

The law recognizes that as children grow and families change, sometimes parenting time needs to be modified along the way. However, take parenting time orders seriously and do not agree to a parenting time order at the early Friend of the Court coordination conference if you do not feel you can live with it for the long haul. As discussed above, when evaluating requests for change of custody or parenting time, courts place a premium on maintaining stability for the child, and changes are not readily granted absent compelling circumstances. Do not agree to a parenting time arrangement based on your understanding that it is only temporary and can always change at the time of the final settlement. The longer a parenting time arrangement is in place, the harder it is to change if things are going reasonably well. It is wisest to look at a temporary order with the same scrutiny as you would a permanent one, as it very well may become just that.

Parenting time is generally modifiable upon showing of good cause or a change in circumstances in accordance with the best interest of the child. Examples of good cause include such things as household relocation, changes in the parents' work schedules, changing educational needs or school districts, remarriage of a parent, abuse, neglect, substance abuse or criminal behavior (on the part of the parent or the child), health or behavioral issues or simply the passage of time, coupled with the child's expressing a desire for more parenting time with the non-custodial parent. Motions for change of parenting time are discussed in greater detail in chapter 10 below.

Parenting time disputes are one of the most common reasons divorced couples return to court after the divorce is final. If you will remember a few basic principles, parenting time can be more positive for you and your children.

Ten Essential Principles for More Positive Parenting Time

1. **Parenting time and support are not dependent on one another.** Remember, child support and parenting time are two different issues. The right to parenting time belongs to the child, and whether the child's parent is receiving child support should not interfere with the child's right to a close relationship with both parents. Likewise, denial of parenting time is not a reason to withhold support.

2. **If you show flexibility and leniency with the other parent, you will receive the same. If you are overly legalistic, expect the same in return.** While it is important to adhere to a parenting time schedule, keep in mind that sometimes work schedules, weather, or other circumstances may present a challenge. Do your best to recognize that parenting time is an important right that belongs to your children, regardless of how good or bad your ex may be at adhering to the parenting time schedule. In most cases flexibility, not rigidity, serves the best interests of the children.

3. **Present parenting time in a positive light to the children.** As you prepare your children to spend time with their other parent, do not show resentment or hesitation. Instead, present it as a positive opportunity. Try to avoid sending the children the message that they must visit with the other parent "because the judge said so."

4. **Clarify expectations regarding food, clothing, medications and other routine aspects of parenting time.** Parenting time will be a far more positive experience if you and your ex are able to discuss and agree on who will provide these things. For example, if parenting time begins at 6:00 PM, discuss in advance who will provide dinner. If your

child requires diapers or formula, discuss in advance who will be providing these necessities.

5. **Establish a preferred method of communication and stick with it.** If you and your ex are comfortable using text messages or phone calls for communicating arrival times, etc., practice some consistency. If you normally text when you are going to be late, don't expect that she will check her office voicemail if you leave a message there. Discuss preferred methods of communication early in your case, develop a plan and stick with it.

6. **It is your job to have your children ready for parenting time and encourage them to go.** Remember that the parenting time provisions in your judgment of divorce are orders, not suggestions. Do not present parenting time as optional to your child, and do not let the child decide if he or she is going to parenting time. If the parenting time provisions are not working, you can always file a motion to modify them.

7. **Do not rely on your child to be a messenger.** This often puts children in an awkward position and can cause conflict between the parents. If you have parenting time concerns that need to be expressed to the other parent, you can always keep a journal in the child's backpack or establish a protocol of emailing each other immediately after parenting time to check in.

8. **There are very few valid excuses for missing parenting time.** As discussed above, parenting time is not optional. Just because the child is sick, has other plans, or does not feel like going to the other parent's house, you cannot unilaterally cancel parenting time. Of course, in the spirit of flexibility, you and the other parent should not hesitate to adjust parenting time schedules if it will serve the children's best interest.

9. **If for some reason you are unable to comply with the parenting time schedule, offer makeup time.** You will build many bridges with your ex if you take the initiative to make things right.

10. **Recognize individual parenting time styles and don't criticize the other parent, especially in the presence of your children.** You may not agree with everything that takes place during your ex's parenting

time. However, unless there is abuse or neglect, which may require you to contact the authorities, try to recognize individual parenting styles. You may feel that your children watch too much television, eat too much junk food, or play too many video games while at the other parent's house. Courts seldom get involved in this type of judgment call, and if you try to change the parenting time schedule or file a parenting time complaint based on differences of parenting style, it may damage your credibility with the judge. If you have concerns about how the children are spending their time, discuss this with your ex. If you cannot agree on these matters, or if you sense that the conflict is getting out of control, it may be time for some co-parenting counseling.

Medical Marijuana and Parenting Time

Since Michigan legalized the use and regulated growing of medical marijuana, the role a parent's use of medical marijuana can play in custody or parenting time has become a topic of controversy. A parent in a custody case may attempt to limit the other parent's time with the child due to the parent's use of medical marijuana. The Medical Marijuana Act offers protection for those who possess a registry identification card.

Michigan's Medical Marijuana Act ("the Act") states in pertinent part:

A qualifying patient who has been issued and possesses a registry identification card shall not be subject to arrest, prosecution, or penalty in any manner, or denied any right or privilege, including but not limited to civil penalty or disciplinary action by a business or occupational or professional licensing board or bureau, for the medical use of marijuana in accordance with this act, provided that that the qualifying patient possesses an amount of marijuana that does not exceed 2.5 ounces of usable marijuana, and, if the qualifying patient has not specified that a primary caregiver will be allowed under state law to cultivate marijuana for the qualifying patient, twelve marijuana plants kept in an enclosed, locked facility. Any incidental amount of seed, stalks, and unusable roots shall also be allowed under state law and shall not be included in this amount. (Michigan Compiled Laws Section 333.26424)

With respect to parenting time, MCL 333.26424(c) states:

(c) A person shall not be denied custody or visitation of a minor for acting in accordance with [the Medical Marijuana Act], unless the person's behavior is such that it creates an unreasonable danger to the minor that can be clearly articulated and substantiated.

The Medical Marijuana statute does not grant to a court the authority to independently determine whether a person is a qualifying patient. All that a person must do to obtain protection under the Act is possess a registration card (Michigan Compiled Laws Section 333.26424(a)). To receive a registry identification card, a "written certification" from a physician is required. This is defined as:

[a] document signed by a physician, stating the patient's debilitating medical condition and stating that, in the physician's professional opinion, the patient is likely to receive therapeutic or palliative benefit from the medical use of marijuana to treat or alleviate the patient's debilitating medical condition or symptoms associated with the debilitating medical condition. (MCL 333.26423(l))

The Act does not define the terms "unreasonable danger" or "articulated and substantiated," and as of the time this book goes to press, our appellate courts have not issued a precedential decision on application of section 4(c). This area of the law is constantly evolving as municipalities throughout the state continue to decriminalize or legalize the recreational use of marijuana.

Because the law surrounding medical marijuana and parenting time is so new and controversial, little is clear. The statute does offer protection but it is not without limits. The court may review evidence to determine whether a person's conduct related to marijuana is for the purpose of treating or alleviating the person's debilitating medical condition or symptoms associated with the condition. Michigan Compiled Laws Section 333.26424(d)(2). If the person's use or possession of marijuana is not for that specific therapeutic purpose, and thus not "in accordance with" the Act, the person is not entitled to rely on the Act's protections. Until this area of the law is better developed, how a court views medical marijuana's impact on parenting time will undoubtedly be influenced by the individual judge's experiences and personal opinion.

Grandparenting Time

Michigan law recognizes the rights of grandparents to visitation with their grandchildren, but only in a few limited circumstances. A grandparent's right to spend time with a grandchild is in most cases derivative of the parent's time with the child. There are, however, a limited number of circumstances where a grandparent can petition the court for grandparenting time. Michigan Compiled Laws Section 722.27b provides that grandparenting time *may* be awarded only under one or more of the following circumstances:

a) "An action for divorce, separate maintenance, or annulment involving the child's parents is pending before the court.

b) The child's parents are divorced, separated under a judgment of separate maintenance, or have had their marriage annulled.

c) The child's parent who is a child of the grandparents is deceased.

d) The child's parents have never been married, they are not residing in the same household, and paternity has been established by the completion of an acknowledgment of parentage […] or by a determination by a court […] that the individual is the father of the child.

e) […] Legal custody of the child has been given to a person other than the child's parent, or the child is placed outside of and does not reside in the home of the parent.

f) In the year preceding the commencement of an action […] for grandparenting time, the grandparent provided an established custodial environment for the child […]." (Michigan Compiled Laws sec. 722.27b)

The existence of one or more of the above situations *does not guarantee* grandparenting time. It merely gives the grandparent the right to file an action for grandparenting time or seek an order in an existing action before a court that has continuing jurisdiction over the child. In such an action, the grandparent must file an affidavit (a sworn statement) setting forth facts supporting the order of grandparenting time. The grandparent must give notice to any party with legal custody of the child. If one of the child's fit parents files an affidavit opposing the grandparenting time, the statute creates a presumption that the parent's decision to deny grandparenting time "does not create a substantial risk of harm to the child's mental, physical, or emotional health." The grandparent then has the duty to rebut such a presumption by proving "[...] by a preponderance of the evidence that the parent's decision to deny grandparenting time creates a substantial risk of harm to the child's mental, physical, or emotional health. [...]" If the grandparent does not overcome the presumption, "[...] the court shall dismiss the complaint or deny the motion."

If both of the child's fit parents file an affidavit opposing the grandparenting time request, the court "*shall* dismiss a complaint or motion seeking an order for grandparenting time [...] (Michigan Compiled Laws section 722.2 7b(4)(a),(b), 722.27b(5)).

In other words, if one parent opposes a grandparent's request for parenting time, the grandparent has a difficult burden of proof. But if *both* parents oppose the request, the motion for grandparenting time will be dismissed without further inquiry. This statute is based on the principle that fit parents have a right to make parenting decisions for their children and their decisions must be granted great deference.

CHAPTER 5

Property Division

"He who dies with the most toys wins."
— SEEN ON A GUY'S T-SHIRT AT A CHILD
SUPPORT SHOW CAUSE HEARING

The law requires that every judgment of divorce contain provisions dividing real and personal property. Real property includes the marital home and any other real estate owned by the parties during the marriage, whether by one or both. Vacation homes, investment properties, timeshares, farmland, vacant land and improvements on the real estate, and the seller's interest in a land contract for property that has been sold are all considered real property. Personal property includes accounts, household contents, vehicles, tools, live animals, antiques and collectibles, and any other movable property. If real or personal property is held as part of a partnership or shares of a corporation, it is still property that will be considered by the court in the final judgment.

The Marital Estate

When you meet with your lawyer in the early stages of your divorce, you will need to provide an accurate inventory of everything you and your spouse have acquired during the marriage. In addition, try to document exactly what was owned by each of you at the time of your marriage. For example, if you married later in life and you both owned a home, furnish your attorney with a description of that real estate, together with any debts owed on it at the time of the marriage. If it is still owned by either of you, whether individually or in joint, your attorney needs to understand the origin of this property. Take an inventory of your household furnishings, and if anything was acquired by either of you prior to the marriage, make a note of it. Also, if anything came to either of you through inheritance or gift from your family, make a note of this. The origin of property owned at the time of the divorce may determine whether it is considered part of the marital estate. If either you or your spouse has received an inheritance, a gift from family or money from a personal injury or workers' compensation settlement, let your attorney know.

I like to use the analogy of a pie when I discuss property settlement with my clients. If the marital estate is represented by the whole of the pie, each of you will receive an equitable portion of that pie. In addition, there may be other assets in your household that fall outside of this pie. This may be considered separate property because it was acquired by either of you prior to the marriage, or if it came to one of you through inheritance or individual gift from a family member. Because the value of the marital estate may fluctuate over time with changes in the market, the court will exercise discretion on what date to value the assets. In the early stages of your divorce, you should make every effort to assist your attorney in placing a value on your assets, so you can begin to envision what the property distribution might look like.

Prenuptial Agreements

If your marriage was a second one for either of you, or if you or your spouse owned significant assets at the time of the marriage, you may have entered into a prenuptial agreement defining the rights of each spouse on death or in a divorce. For the most part, prenuptial agreements are enforceable, provided they meet certain criteria.

First, a prenuptial agreement must fully disclose all material facts regarding the property held by each prospective spouse and valuation of same at the time of marriage. Most commonly, this is done through a schedule of assets and liabilities incorporated into the agreement.

Second, a prenuptial agreement is more likely to be enforced by the court if both parties were represented by attorneys at the time the agreement was made. An enforceable agreement will verify that the parties have been counseled regarding what property rights each of them would have in the assets of the other, and what rights are being waived by entering into the agreement. Ideally, the agreement should be signed in the presence of attorneys for both spouses affirming full disclosure.

There are numerous other factors that can come into play if one party tries to invalidate a prenuptial agreement. There may be co-mingling of assets during the marriage, which one spouse may argue has defeated the purpose of the agreement. One spouse may argue that he or she was coerced into signing a prenuptial agreement, or that he or she did not understand the document. Whatever the case, if you and your spouse entered into a prenuptial agreement, be sure to get a copy of it to your attorney as soon as possible. If you plan to rely on such an agreement, it must be attached to the complaint for divorce or specifically referenced in it. Have your attorney carefully review the agreement and provide you with an opinion early in your case as to its enforceability, as this may drastically affect the outcome of the property division and spousal support award.

The Rule of Equitable Division

Michigan is a marital property state, meaning that property in the marital estate is subject to *equitable* division, which in most cases, but not all, means *equal* division. Property outside the marital estate, sometimes called separate property, is usually awarded to the party who owns it. Sometimes the issue of whether a particular asset constitutes separate property is debated by the attorneys and must be settled by the court. Under certain circumstances separate property can be considered part of the marital estate, subject to division. The most common way this occurs is when the non-owner spouse is able to prove that he or she contributed to the "acquisition, improvement, or accumulation" of the asset (see Michigan Compiled Laws section 552.401), or in the case where, considering all the circumstances, the non-owning spouse is in need of support, and assets in the marital estate are not sufficient to provide for this (See Michigan Compiled Laws section 552.23). A common example of the first scenario is when a couple acquires a piece of real estate, often a recreational property such as a lakefront cottage, as an inheritance from one spouse's family. During the marriage, they enjoy family vacations at the property for many years. Of course, with the benefits of ownership come the burdens. Over the years, they remodel and expand the cottage, maintain it, landscape, improve the waterfront, and pay significant non-homestead taxes, all financed with marital funds and labor. Twenty years later, the little fishing cabin they inherited from Uncle Martin is now a sprawling year-round waterfront home worth a million dollars. Under this scenario, the non-owning spouse would likely convince the court that she meets the statutory requirement of having contributed to the asset's improvement or accumulation. Therefore, this property will most likely be equitably divided. In many cases, the spouse who brought the asset into the marriage by means of inheritance may receive a larger portion of the asset, but the appreciation, which may be due in part to joint efforts and financing, may be equally divided.

The second scenario under which separate property may be awarded to the non-owning spouse is when the marital estate is insufficient for that spouse's "suitable support." Spousal support is discussed below. In some cases, for example, where the parties are retired, there may be no current earnings stream to pay spousal support. In that case, the court may look to separate property assets and award them to the non-owning spouse as a means of support.

Real Estate

Real estate, and in particular the marital home, is often the most valuable asset a couple owns. During the real estate crash beginning in the late 2000s, ownership of real estate presented a significant obstacle to settling many divorces, as people found themselves owing more on their mortgages than their homes were worth. This often made it difficult to divide the mortgage debt and sometimes necessitated couples owning real estate together or living together in the marital home for months or even years after the divorce.

While real estate values in many parts of our state have recovered some, the market remains unpredictable. People still have differing and sometimes unrealistic perceptions of what their homes are worth. For this reason, it is imperative that you hire a licensed real estate appraiser in the early stages of your divorce to help you develop realistic expectations of what will happen with your home and any other real estate you own in the final settlement. Many people ask me if a free market analysis, offered by some realtors, will suffice. While it may provide general information on potential asking price, do not rely solely on a market analysis as evidence of value. These opinions vary greatly from broker to broker and are of limited evidentiary value if your case goes to trial. Only a licensed appraiser is qualified to testify on the issue of value. I have seen appraisals deviate as much as 40% from a market analysis. If you have a mortgage on your home, you must arm yourself with a realistic idea of what your net equity is before you begin to negotiate a settlement. It is also a good idea to explore whether you or your spouse will be able to refinance the mortgage in one of your names alone if either of you decides to keep the house.

There are many ways equity in real estate can be divided. The home can be sold, and the proceeds split on an equitable basis. Or, if one spouse wants to keep the home, if there is equity, that spouse can in many cases buy out the equity of the other. To illustrate, consider the example of William and Mary, who have been married for 25 years. They have lived in their present home for 10 years, and their current mortgage balance is $110,000. William wants to stay in the house, and Mary has agreed that she will find a place of her own after the divorce is final. William's attorney hired an appraiser, who values the home at $257,000. A bit of simple math shows their net equity:

Home value:	$257,000
Less mortgage balance:	($110,000)
Net equity:	$147,000
Mary and William's equity:	$73,500 each

All other things being equal, William and Mary each have $73,500 in equity. In order to assess settlement possibilities, William should sit down with his lawyer and determine, if he keeps the house, will he be able to pay Mary her $73,500 to buy her out? Does he have the cash to do this? If so, all he needs to do is get Mary released from the mortgage liability and give her the cash, with no need to pull any equity out of the home.

Occasionally, if the party who wants to keep the home is creditworthy, a lender will simply grant a release from the mortgage debt to the spouse who is not keeping the home. More often than not, though, the lender will require William to refinance the home in his sole name. If he determines he will need to buy out Mary's entire interest and finance this, he would need to independently qualify for a new mortgage in the amount of $183,500. Sometimes people cannot qualify for a new mortgage on their own credit following divorce. For example, if William and Mary were both employed, with Mary earning as much as or more than William, in that instance, William might not be able to refinance the house based on his income alone. This can present practical difficulties when trying to settle a case like this.

An alternative to new mortgage financing is known as the "hold harmless" arrangement. It is often used when divorcing couples have little equity in a home, or if the spouse retaining the home simply cannot qualify to refinance the mortgage. Under this arrangement, the judgment provides that the parties remain jointly on the mortgage, with the party keeping the home promising to pay it on a timely basis and assuming all liability for the debt. There may be a delay built into the arrangement whereby the buyout occurs at the time of refinancing. A word of warning, though: If the party keeping the house does not make the mortgage payments, it will affect the credit of the other ex-spouse, and if there is a foreclosure, the asset may be lost entirely. And, just to be clear, the mortgage company will continue to hold both William and Mary liable for any deficiency (shortfall between what is owed and the value of the property) and does not care what the judgment of divorce says. For this reason, it is important that if you decide to incorporate a "hold harmless" in your judgment of divorce, ask your lawyer to include other mechanisms for enforcement if your ex does not make the mortgage payments. At a minimum, there should be a deadline of at most a couple of years by which the spouse owning the home must either refinance or sell it. The judgment should also provide that the court retains continuing jurisdiction to resolve any disputes over the mortgage, including an award of attorney fees to the non-offending party if going to court is required. And remember, if your judgment of divorce incorporates a "hold harmless", the spouse who is walking away from the home will still be jointly liable on the mortgage, which impacts her credit rating and debt to income ratio until the mortgage is refinanced. So if you or your soon-to-be ex are planning on buying a new home soon after the divorce, the "hold harmless" simply may not work for you.

There are many creative ways to handle division of real property, especially if there is substantial equity. If, for example, the home is paid for and the spouse keeping the home does not want to take out a new mortgage to buy out the other spouse's equity, he could equalize this through giving her a greater share of other assets, such as retirement accounts. Sometimes when divorcing couples have minor children they choose to keep the house in joint ownership until the children have grown, and the judgment of divorce incorporates a formula for division of the proceeds of sale in the future. Of course, this type of arrangement carries some risk, since no one can predict what the real estate market will do. It also requires that the cost of carrying the marital home be allocated on an equitable basis. With a little creativity, joint ownership can work. However I recommend it only for those couples who have an unusually amicable relationship after the divorce.

Ask your attorney to explore all of the scenarios for division of real property. The sooner you obtain an appraisal, the better position you will be in to assess your options.

Personal Property

Anything you own that is not attached to the real estate is considered personal property. This includes:

- household furnishings and contents;
- cash accounts;
- vehicles and watercraft;
- tools;
- antiques and collectibles;
- accounts receivable;
- stocks, bonds, mutual funds and investment accounts;
- shares in closely held corporations, partnerships or limited liability company memberships;
- businesses or professional practices;
- sporting equipment, guns;
- live animals, pets;
- airline frequent flyer miles or travel bonus points;
- timeshares or club memberships;
- stock options;
- employee stock ownership plans;
- intellectual property such as patents, trademarks, copyrights;
- jewelry and personal effects.

As discussed above, it is important to take a careful inventory of all personal property early in your divorce proceeding. If your household furnishings consist of typical used furniture, it is not always necessary to have an appraisal. If you and your future ex are communicating productively, it may be possible to sit down together and draw up a list of household content division without any specific valuation. However, if you have furnishings of extraordinary value, such as heirlooms or collectible items, it may be necessary to have a personal property valuation. Your lawyer likely has a relationship with an appraiser, and if not you can probably find one in the phone book or online. Most estate sale or auctioneer services offer appraisals tailored to helping people settle divorces.

Sometimes when couples separate for a period of time prior to filing for divorce, they have already physically divided their belongings when one of them moves out, which proves helpful in the settlement. If a couple has been separated for awhile, agreeing on the personal property split, the final judgment of divorce might say something as simple as "the parties have divided all personal property and shall retain all items in their respective possession and control." If the spouses are still residing together at the time of entry of judgment, it may be necessary to have an itemized list attached as an exhibit to the judgment of divorce.

As a general rule, judges do not want to get involved in helping people decide who gets the pots and pans. The majority of my clients are able to resolve personal property through direct negotiation early in the proceedings. In the event they are not able to do this, I ask them to submit a list of everything in the house. I will then ask them to designate on that list what they want to keep, after which the list is forwarded to opposing counsel. If there are disputed items on the list that cannot be settled, sometimes a meeting with both parties and their attorneys is an effective means of resolving the remaining items. If such a meeting does not work, and items remain in dispute, I have seen the issue resolved by writing the disputed items on slips of paper, placing them in a hat and having a blind draw.

When looking at the value of items, remember that the courts consider current cash value, not original cost or replacement value when dividing personal property. The judge does not care that your mother paid $360 for the VCR in your basement in 1986. If the item will bring you five bucks at a garage sale, that it is what it is worth for property settlement purposes.

In addition to tangible personal property, other items, such as accounts, must be allocated in the judgment of divorce. Sometimes liquid accounts can be closed and the proceeds divided prior to the judgment of divorce, which is sometimes necessary to pay attorney fees or living expenses.

Professional Degrees

A professional credential such as a medical or law degree, especially in cases where it enables the holder of the degree to earn significant income, is sometimes considered a marital asset subject to valuation and equitable division, just like any other property accumulated during the marriage. The most compelling case for division of the value of a professional degree is presented in situations where one spouse has assisted the other in a concerted family effort to obtain the degree, through assistance with payment of tuition and related expenses or household services. Be sure to clearly summarize the history leading up to the achievement of any professional degrees by you or your spouse for your attorney. Was the degree obtained during the marriage or before? What was the cost of the required course work? Are you and your spouse in debt due to acquisition of this degree? If the debt was previously repaid, was that done with marital funds? The more history you can provide, the more accurate a picture your attorney can give you concerning whether this professional credential will be considered a marital asset.

Companion Animals

If you have pets in your household, they are considered personal property and should not be overlooked in the judgment of divorce. In the vast majority of cases, one spouse or the other has more emotional attachment to the animal, and this is usually easy to determine. If the animal is of extraordinary value, such as a registered show dog or a racehorse, the animal should be appraised by an expert, and its value considered in the property distribution. As is often the case, the children may be attached to a pet, and in this case the judge would likely award the pet to the party who has custody of the children. I have seen creative arrangements whereby possession of the pet parallels custody of the children; when the children are with Dad, the pet is with Dad, and vice versa. Having a pet travel with the children to parenting time may help them feel more at home when spending time with the noncustodial parent. However, the law is clear that a pet is personal property, so do not expect the court to get involved in establishing "pet parenting time".

Enforcement of Property Division

After the judgment of divorce enters, there will be some exchange of property. You may need to transfer vehicle titles or move property out of the marital home. If the home is being sold, the parties will need to cooperate to get it listed and cover expenses of sale. There may be a cash settlement due one of the parties, and retirement assets will be divided.

If you are concerned about your ex's ability or willingness to comply with the property settlement terms of your judgment for any reason, discuss this with your attorney. In cases where there is a pattern of deceit or fraudulent behavior on the part of one or both parties, it is especially important that the attorneys incorporate language in the judgment of divorce to give it some teeth and provide for compensation if one party fails to comply. One method of assuring compliance is to incorporate an attorney fee provision saying that if one of the parties fails to comply with any provision of the judgment of divorce, the other party may petition the court to enforce or modify the judgment to obtain compliance. Courts will routinely enforce language that compels the noncompliant party to pay the other party's attorney fees necessitated by the noncompliance. The judgment of divorce may also grant one party a lien on the assets of the other, pending satisfaction of the property settlement terms. If you are at all concerned that your ex may not comply with the judgment, take the time to discuss this with your attorney and ask her to include enforcement remedies in your judgment.

Division of Retirement Assets

Retirement accounts, including pensions, 401(k)s, IRAs, 403(b)s, and other investment plans, are in most cases considered marital assets subject to division in divorce. Retirement accounts are often the most valuable asset in the marital estate and should not be overlooked. Early in your case, ask your attorney to send a discovery request to opposing counsel asking your spouse to disclose all retirement assets owned. Once the disclosure is received, your attorney should subpoena the retirement account statements directly from the employer. I am often surprised at how little the spouses in divorce cases know about the other's retirement assets. Many times a spouse has pensions or other accounts from previous employers of which my client is completely unaware. If you or your spouse had any retirement accounts prior to the marriage, try to obtain an account statement from at or near the time of the marriage so your attorney can determine what part of the account may be a premarital asset and therefore not subject to division.

There are many different types of retirement plans available. Many of these, including 401(k)s and traditional pension plans, are governed by a federal statute known as ERISA, the Employee Retirement and Investment Securities Act. Other retirement plans, such as military pensions and state teacher retirement board plans, are governed by additional state or federal statutes. The details of these plans are many and beyond the scope of this book.

When you first consult with your divorce attorney and discuss the fee agreement, you should ask her if she has expertise in division of retirement assets, and if preparation of the required orders is part of the fee agreement. If your attorney does not possess specific expertise in division of retirement assets, request a referral to an attorney who specializes in this area, especially if you have a military or government pension, or something other than a standard 401(k) or IRA.

Early in your divorce, your attorney should request copies of plan documents from each retirement plan administrator. Your attorney will look carefully at statements for each retirement account and assist you in determining what portion of these accounts should be awarded to you or your spouse as part of the final settlement. Assuming all the retirement accounts have been accrued during the marriage, the general rule of equitable property division discussed above applies. If a percentage of these accounts accrued prior to the marriage, your attorney should assess what portion of the accounts is marital. This can be a somewhat detailed calculation, and your attorney may seek the advice of a pension valuation expert, often a certified public accountant or actuary who specializes in valuation of retirement assets. Simply put, look at the current balance of the account as compared with the balance at the time of the marriage. The difference between these two balances constitutes the "marital portion" of the account, which is then equitably divided between the spouses. If the two of you have several retirement accounts between you, as is often the case, it may be appropriate to equalize the accounts through a single transfer.

Many retirement accounts, primarily those governed by ERISA as discussed above, are subject to special requirements in order to avoid the transfer being deemed an early distribution subject to taxes and penalties. For this reason, your attorney (or a specialist in retirement asset division) will need to prepare a Qualified Domestic Relations Order, sometimes referred to as a QDRO (say "Quadro"). Every retirement plan has its own requirements governing the preparation and approval of QDROs. There is often a fee associated with transfer of retirement accounts, sometimes as much as $250 per hour for review and communication by the plan administrator. Your attorney should contact your employer to obtain information on the QDRO approval process before the judgment of divorce is entered. Many retirement plans offer template QDROs to assist counsel in preparing the orders. These templates should serve only as a guide, and should not replace your attorney's legal judgment on the appropriateness of the order.

If you will be receiving a portion of your spouse's retirement assets as part of the divorce settlement, try to predict your financial needs following the divorce and determine whether you will need to utilize any of this asset for daily living expenses, to purchase a home, or to pay off debt. If you plan to do this rather than allowing the retirement assets to remain in a tax-deferred plan such as a rollover IRA, consult with a tax professional, preferably a CPA, regarding how to structure the transfer to minimize taxes or penalties. You may be able to characterize withdrawals from your portion of the retirement assets as hardship withdrawals or other exemptions to the penalty provisions.

You should also ask your tax and investment professional if it would be advisable to leave the portion of the retirement assets you are receiving invested with the same company, as opposed to opening a new account with a different financial institution. If you decide to move the account to a new institution, perhaps with a financial advisor with whom you have a relationship, you should prepare for this prior to entry of your judgment of divorce by establishing a rollover IRA or similar account to receive the funds.

Sometimes it takes a couple of months to transfer the retirement assets. If you anticipate needing the money immediately, tell your attorney to start preparing the QDRO or refer your matter to a specialist in this area before the judgment of divorce is entered. There are several stages to the process; do not be surprised if it takes between two and six months to finalize the transfer. Your attorney first needs to communicate with the employer and obtain the contact information for the plan administrator. She will then need to contact the plan administrator and obtain guidelines for approval of QDROs. Once it is determined what portion of your spouse's account you will be receiving, your attorney will need to prepare the QDRO and have it approved by the plan administrator. Once that is done, opposing counsel must review and approve it. Only then can your attorney submit a signed original of the QDRO to the court. This can be entered at the time of the judgment of divorce or shortly thereafter. Sometimes it takes a couple of weeks for the court to actually enter the order once it is submitted. When your attorney receives the certified copy of the QDRO, she will then submit it to the plan administrator, and a portion of the account will be set aside pending instruction from you on how you want it transferred. Many plan administrators require a signed letter of instruction from the recipient of the funds and the attorney, as well as a certified copy of the judgment of divorce, before the transfer can occur. This can be a tedious process, so be sure to discuss estimated fees with your attorney or whoever is preparing the necessary orders to avoid any unpleasant surprises.

Allocation of Debt

Unless you are among the fortunate few who have no marital debt, allocation of debts will be an issue you will need to deal with. During your initial meeting with your attorney, provide detailed information concerning any debts you and your spouse have incurred prior to or during the marriage. Your attorney should send interrogatories to opposing counsel inquiring as to all debts owed by you and your spouse. Be sure to cancel any joint credit cards, home equity lines of credit, overdraft protection lines of credit on any checking accounts, and any other potential avenues for incurring additional debt.

Once you have compiled a detailed schedule of debts, be sure to ascertain whether the accounts are individual or joint. Sometimes one spouse has a credit card that the other does not even know about, and both spouses may be jointly liable on the debt. As discussed above under information gathering, run credit reports early in the process and just before entry of judgment of divorce to make sure you are not missing any debts. There may be some debts that do not show up in credit reports. Your spouse may owe money on a land contract that has not been recorded. He may owe money to a relative, may have incurred gambling debts, or have other unsecured obligations. Your attorney can flesh these out through discovery.

In an ideal world, joint debts will be paid off prior to entry of the judgment of divorce. However, this is not always possible. If, for example, a couple has a $10,000 balance on a joint credit card and no assets to pay the debt, the judgment of divorce may require one of the parties to make the payment until paid in full. If this is the case, the judgment should provide that the one responsible for paying the debt must indemnify the other from any liability for the debt. Your attorney should incorporate language providing that if your ex does not pay on the joint obligation as required, you can go back to court for post-judgment relief. This may include the right to spousal support to compensate you for your ex's failure to comply, as well as attorney fees.

Do not for one minute believe that you can exonerate yourself from paying a joint debt by allocating that debt to your spouse in the judgment of divorce. The creditor does not care what the judgment says. You will still be liable for timely payments, and if your ex does not comply with payment obligations, your credit will be damaged, and you could be sued by the creditor. Therefore, as is the case with mortgage debt, I recommend "hold harmless" provisions only as a last resort.

Bankruptcy and Divorce

If you and your spouse have accumulated significant marital debt, to the extent you are concerned about your ability to repay it, talk to your attorney about bankruptcy before you file for divorce. If you are thinking about filing for bankruptcy, be aware that this may cause a significant delay in your divorce. When one divorcing party files a bankruptcy petition, the bankruptcy court issues an "automatic stay", which essentially freezes a divorce proceeding. If you have a pending trial date in your divorce and the court receives notice of a bankruptcy petition, the trial cannot go forward.

Filing joint bankruptcy with your spouse prior to filing for divorce may entitle you to discharge some or all of your joint debt, which can make it much easier to settle your divorce and may provide a fresh start for both of you.

Sometimes one of the parties to a divorce files for bankruptcy, but the other chooses not to. If this is a possibility in your case, proceed with caution, for if you are jointly liable on debts such as credit cards, car payments, a mortgage, etc., and your spouse files for bankruptcy after the divorce, she may obtain discharge for her liability on debts that are joint with you. If this happens, you can be stuck holding the bag for her portion of the debt, even if the judgment of divorce says otherwise. For this reason, it is standard practice for attorneys to incorporate anti-bankruptcy language in the judgment of divorce. This provides that the payment of debt allocated in the judgment is a function of family support, and is therefore non-dischargeable in bankruptcy, just like spousal support and child support. This provision can also vest the court with power to order spousal support in the event one of the spouses is unfairly saddled with debt after the other files for bankruptcy. Be sure to discuss this option with your attorney and ask him to incorporate bankruptcy protection in your judgment.

Tax Considerations

Divorce can significantly impact your income taxes. Before finalizing your divorce, consult with a tax professional concerning what to expect so there are no surprises come tax time. If you are the recipient of spousal support, do not forget that the periodic payments are taxable income. Conversely, if you are paying spousal support, the payments are in most cases deductible. Child support is generally neither deductible nor taxable as income. Do not count on deducting payments made in fulfillment of property settlement, as these are generally not deductible. Most family law attorneys will readily admit that they are not tax specialists and will likely encourage you to seek outside tax advice.

The judgment of divorce will also govern division of tax exemptions between you and your ex-spouse. The courts tend to award the tax exemptions to the custodial parent or equally distribute available exemptions for children between the parties, absent a good reason to do otherwise. While in most cases equal division of exemptions is an equitable arrangement, in some situations it may be advantageous for one party to claim more of the exemptions; for instance, if one party's income is much greater than the other's. A tax professional can assist you in running the various scenarios based on anticipated incomes. If you receive such advice, be sure to communicate it to your attorney, who can take it into consideration when settling your case.

Consult with your tax professional concerning filing status. In most cases, it is advantageous to file married and jointly. For this reason, people divorcing near the end of the year sometimes choose to wait until the first of the new year to finalize the divorce in order to file jointly. Most courts are willing to delay entry of the divorce judgment to facilitate this.

Divorce can change the tax landscape dramatically. Therefore, it is imperative that you seek advice from a tax professional, and the sooner the better.

CHAPTER 6

Financial Support

> "My favorite things in life don't cost any money. It's really
> clear that the most precious resource we all have is time."
>
> — STEVE JOBS

Child Support

Every child has an inherent right to receive support from his or her natural or adoptive parents. Our courts calculate support based on the Michigan Child Support Formula developed by the Friend of the Court Bureau and updated for economic changes. You can find the Michigan Child Support Manual online at www.courts.mi.gov.

If you have minor children at the time of your divorce, you will either pay or receive support for them. The court orders child support consisting of not only cash payment, but apportionment of healthcare expenses, health insurance premiums and childcare costs.

The courts are authorized to "enter orders concerning the care, custody, and support of the minor children of the parties during the pendency of the action" (Michigan Compiled Laws Section 552.15). The court will probably enter a temporary support order early in your divorce. As with other temporary orders, if the order is entered on an *ex parte* basis, either by motion of one party or on recommendation of the Friend of the Court, the court will issue a notice of the right to object to the order. If one of the parties files an objection to the temporary support order, the court will schedule a hearing, at which the judge will either affirm or modify the order.

In many cases, the payor of support falls into arrears early on due to the delay between filing the complaint for divorce and entry of the first support order. Support generally begins at the date of filing the complaint for divorce, and if the temporary order does not take effect until 4 to 6 weeks after the complaint is filed, the payor will be faced with a significant arrearage. When one parent pays support directly to the other during this lag time, the parent making the payment should obtain a written receipt from the other and furnish this to the Friend of the Court, preferably prior to or at the coordination conference. This enables the Friend of the Court to give the payor credit against arrearages.

In every case with minor children, the judgment of divorce must incorporate a child support order utilizing the uniform child support forms issued by the state. Most attorneys and the Friend of the Court utilize software programs to calculate child support. These are available through Margin Soft, publisher of Support 2015, developed by attorney Craig Ross of Ann Arbor, Michigan (www.marginsoft.com) or through Springfield Publications , which produces the Child Support and Alimony prognosticator (www.sppub.com).

Every child support order must incorporate a written support calculation based on the Michigan Support Formula. If the order deviates from the formula, it must identify what support would be if the formula is applied, as compared to the deviation.

Deviation from the Support Formula

The courts nearly always award child support consistent with the Michigan Child Support Formula. If the court determines that application of the formula would be unjust, the support order may deviate from it. However, if there is a deviation, the support order must specifically state why it is deviating from the support guidelines. The Michigan Child Support Formula sets forth numerous grounds for deviation from the formula. In addition, where the parents agree to deviate, and have set forth facts in support of that deviation, the court may enter support based upon the agreement.

The grounds for deviation listed in sec. 1.04 of the Michigan Child Support Formula are as follows:

(1) The child has special needs. (2) The child has extraordinary educational expenses. (3) A parent is a minor. (4) The child's residence income is below the threshold to qualify for public assistance, and at least one parent has sufficient income to pay additional support that will raise the child's standard of living above the public assistance threshold. (5) A parent has a reduction in the income available to support a child due to extraordinary levels of jointly accumulated debt. (6) The court awards property in lieu of support for the benefit of the child. (7) A parent is incarcerated with minimal or no income or assets. (8) A parent has incurred, or is likely to incur, extraordinary medical expenses for either that parent or a dependent. (9) A parent earns an income of a magnitude not fully taken into consideration by the formula. (10) A parent receives bonus income in varying amounts or at irregular intervals. (11) Someone other than the parent can supply reasonable and appropriate health care coverage. (12) A parent provides substantially all the support for a stepchild, and the stepchild's parents earn no income and are unable to earn income. (13) A child earns an extraordinary income. (14) The court orders a parent to pay taxes, mortgage installments, home insurance premiums, telephone or utility bills, etc. before entry of a final judgment or order. (15) A parent must pay significant amounts of restitution, fines, fees, or costs associated with that parent's conviction or incarceration for a crime other than those related to failing to support children, or a crime against a child in the current case or that child's sibling, other parent, or custodian. (16) A parent makes payments to a bankruptcy plan or has debt discharged, when either significantly impacts the monies that parent has available to pay support. (17) A parent provides a substantial amount of a child's

day-time care and directly contributes toward a significantly greater share of the child's costs than those reflected by the overnights used to calculate the offset for parental time. (18) A child in the custody of a third-party recipient spends a significant number of overnights with the payor that causes a significant savings in the third party's expenses. (19) The court ordered non-modifiable spousal support paid between the parents before October 2004. (20) When a parent's share of net child care expenses exceeds 50 percent of that parent's base support obligation calculated under §3.02 before applying the parental time offset. (21) Any other factor the court deems relevant to the best interests of a child.

Determining Income

When you first meet with your attorney, be sure to bring copies of income information for both you and your spouse. Try to develop a realistic picture of what the parenting time plan might look like, as the number of overnights awarded to each parent will have a significant impact on child support. If you or your spouse has health insurance, either individually or through your employer, you will need to determine how much it costs to have the children on the insurance policy. Most employers will tell you exactly how much extra is being withheld from your check each month to cover your children.

Childcare Expense

If you or your spouse is paying childcare, furnish your attorney and the Friend of the Court with the childcare schedule and a breakdown of the expenses you incur, as this expenditure is also taken into consideration when calculating child support. The parent paying for daycare will receive a credit toward child support for these expenses. If daycare expenses are sporadic, they can either be paid directly by the parties in proportion to their respective incomes, or the childcare expense credit can be calculated utilizing the average daycare expense spread over the year. For example, some people require weekly daycare for the children in the summer only, when the children are not in school. When this is the case, the total amount expended can be averaged out over the year and included in the monthly support payments year round.

Medical Expenses and Health Insurance

The uniform child support order must address medical expenses. The custodial parent is required by law to pay the first $357 per child of uninsured medical expenses (referred to as "ordinary medical") before expenses can be apportioned between the parties. The order assigns a percentage of uninsured medical expenses above the ordinary medical threshold to each party based on their proportionate incomes. The parents are required to keep track of medical expenditures and in most cases will settle up between themselves for their respective percentages of uninsured medical expenses.

The support order will also address whether one or both parents are required to carry health insurance on the minor children. As a general rule, a parent is required to carry the children on his or her insurance if insurance is available as a benefit of employment at a cost of not more than 5% of gross pay.

Income from Self-Employment

If you or your spouse is self-employed, calculation of child support can present a challenge. Fringe benefits such as cell phones, computers, company cars, travel expenses, etc. may be counted as income in setting support, so make sure your attorney and the Friend of the Court know about these perks. In setting support, the court will look at the amount of money actually available to pay support. In many cases, this is accurately reflected on the income tax documents. However, in some circumstances, the tax documents are not all that should be used in determining how much income is actually available to pay support. As your case progresses, your attorney will want to do some discovery, including examination of banking records, employment records, and corporate documents to obtain an accurate picture of how much income is actually available for support.

Self-employed individuals unfortunately have many opportunities to manipulate their incomes to minimize child support if they wish to do so. For example, a small business owner can defer deposits or collections of receivables at year-end and wait until the following year to account for them in an effort to show less income for the current year, thereby minimizing income available for support. If your spouse works in a cash business such as running a restaurant or bar, or in a building trade enabling him to take on side jobs for payment "under the table," it can be extremely difficult to verify actual income. A business owner in control of daily cash flow can choose noncash methods of compensation such as a company vehicle, a fuel card, travel expenses, meals, etc. If you suspect that your spouse is utilizing dishonest tactics to minimize income for child support purposes, it may be advantageous to retain a forensic accountant to review the pertinent business and personal banking records to determine actual income for child support purposes. A person may, of course, receive some noncash compensation for no improper motive. Whether the income is deliberately concealed for purposes of avoiding child support or simply as a means of savvy tax planning, it is important to obtain a complete picture of actual income. While a financial review by an accountant can be an expensive undertaking, it may be the only accurate way to establish actual income. I have seen numerous instances in my law practice where a self-employed spouse claims a meager salary for tax purposes as well as child support calculation, yet resides in a luxurious home, drives the finest vehicles, and spares no expense when it comes to family vacations, clothing and luxury items. In these situations, thorough document discovery and review by an accountant is a worthwhile investment, which in some cases reveals hidden income.

When you first meet with the Friend of the Court for a coordination conference, you and your spouse will be required to produce income information. The Friend of the Court may require you to bring your recent pay stub, W-2, and tax forms for the current year and the previous year. You will be required to produce information on available health insurance through your employer.

If you are receiving any government benefits such as food stamps, Medicaid or cash assistance, the Friend of the Court will need to know about this, as it must adhere strictly to the Child Support Guidelines when a child is benefitting from state assistance.

Imputation of Income

Sometimes the courts will impute income to a party who is voluntarily under-employed or unemployed. In these cases, support may be calculated as if the parent is earning what the court believes the parent is capable of. The court will try to determine if there is an "unexercised ability to earn" (2013 MCSF 2.01(G)), and if the parent actually has potential income but for some reason is not exercising his or her full earning power. Imputation of income can be a touchy subject. The stay-at-home spouse may have limited earning capacity due to the fact that she has stayed home for years caring for the children while the other spouse was out advancing his career. The working spouse may express resentment toward the stay-at-home spouse, insinuating a lack of motivation or sheer laziness. In deciding whether to impute income, the court will look at the party's health, educational level, and past earnings history. In many cases, if one spouse has been staying at home and caring for the children, if that spouse were to return to the workforce in an entry-level position, the cost of childcare would partially, or in some cases, completely offset the wages the parent would earn. Therefore, courts may be reluctant to impute income to a parent who has been staying at home with the children, unless that parent has better than entry-level earning power. A more realistic approach might be to provide rehabilitative alimony for the first couple of years to enhance that parent's education or job training before imputing any income.

Bonus Income

If you or your spouse receives performance bonuses, discuss this with your attorney and with the Friend of the Court. Sometimes performance bonuses can vary dramatically from year to year. In certain cases, the courts will set support based upon the total income received the prior year, even if it includes bonuses. If bonuses are not received the following year, support may be adjusted accordingly. One way to prevent this fluctuation is to incorporate a percentage of bonus income provision in the child support order so that when one of the parties receives a bonus, he or she is required to report it to the other parent and the Friend of the Court and pay additional support in a lump sum based on a percentage of the bonus received.

To understand how bonus income might be treated in the support calculation, look at compensation history over a period of several years. If bonus compensation follows a predictable trend, you can easily calculate support based on projected bonuses. However, if bonuses are sporadic based on performance or economic conditions, the percentage of bonuses received at year-end might be the preferable method. The support calculation software discussed above contains a bonus calculation tool that can be helpful under many circumstances.

Entry and Enforcement of Support Orders: Working With the Friend of the Court

The courts require that all child support orders be entered on the latest version of a uniform support order, with children's names, dates of birth and number of overnights with each parent listed. The order will set an amount of base support calculated by comparison of the parents' incomes and the number of overnights. If one or both parents are paying childcare expense, the total expense will be apportioned through an adjustment to support based on the ratio of incomes.

Child support orders are most often paid through an order of income withholding which is served on the employer, obligating it to withhold support each pay period from the payor's wages. If the payor is self-employed, in many cases it is up to the payor to make direct payment through the Friend of the Court. If the payor is behind on support, the state can intercept tax refunds. The courts have broad authority to enforce the payment of support, and can suspend a delinquent payor's occupational and driver licenses.

When a new divorce case is filed, support is payable from the date of filing forward. In nearly all cases, the recipient of support does not receive the first payment until several weeks after the case is filed, as it may take several weeks for the court to issue its first child support order, often in conjunction with the Friend of the Court coordination conference. Even then, the paperwork must be processed by the payor's employer and the State Disbursement Unit in Lansing before support begins to flow. Therefore, if you are the payor of support, you will likely find yourself several weeks in arrears at the time the first child support payment is made. You will not be required to pay the arrearage all at once, as the child support formula requires a small percentage of any arrearages to be tacked onto the amount you pay each month until the arrearage is satisfied. Do not expect to avoid arrearages by paying support to your spouse directly during the early weeks unless you have a specific agreement in place with the Friend of the Court office to account for this. If your worker will agree, you can make direct payments through the Friend of the Court office to prevent arrearages from accruing. In most cases, the Friend of the Court will see that you receive credit for properly documented payments. However, do not simply take it for granted that you will receive credit. If possible, meet with your assigned worker early on to address the situation and confirm in writing any payments you make.

If a parent falls behind on support, on motion by the Friend of the Court or the opposing party, the court may issue an order to show cause why the party should not be found in contempt of court for failing to comply with the support order. If found in contempt, a party can be fined or sentenced to jail. If you receive an order to show cause, do not ignore it. You must appear at the hearing, or you may be held in contempt of court, and a bench warrant can be issued for your arrest. Most of the time, the Friend of the Court will work with you to resolve support arrearages before a show cause is ordered. If you fall behind on support, be sure to contact the Friend of the Court and if you have a change in employment, let your Friend of the Court worker know immediately, as support is always modifiable on showing of a change in circumstances.

Sometimes the parties choose to opt out of Friend of the Court services. In cases involving domestic violence or unequal bargaining power, or where the parties or children receive public assistance, Friend of the Court services are mandatory and people are not allowed to opt out. If you and your spouse both agree to opt out, you will first need to file an advice of rights form. Either party may opt back into Friend of the Court services at any time.

Spousal Support

Spousal support, also called alimony, is one of the most frequently litigated issues in divorce, for a number of reasons. First, it is often difficult for a spouse to comprehend supporting the soon-to-be ex after the marriage ends when in many cases the spouse asking for support is the one wanting to end the marriage, sometimes for no apparent reason, or for one perceived by the potential payor of spousal support as unjust or immoral. In other cases, spousal support may be perceived as punitive, when that is not its true purpose.

The Internet has given rise to many misperceptions regarding spousal support, the most common of these being that alimony is dead; that spousal support is only ordered against the at-fault party; that spousal support runs forever; that spousal support is always awarded against the man and in favor of the woman; and the list goes on. Spousal support determinations tend to be largely subjective, often influenced by a judge's own personal convictions or biases. Therefore attorneys may struggle to determine just how much spousal support the judge will order. The courts do recognize spousal support guidelines, but these are just that—guidelines—and unlike the child support formula, they are not mandatory. The guidelines, which are incorporated in the support calculation software programs discussed in the Child Support section above, are based on five of the most readily quantified factors discussed below: Length of the marriage; disparity in spouses' earning powers; education; ages of the parties; and whether the recipient was the primary care provider for the children. The remaining, more subjective factors are addressed on a case-by-case basis.

The statute governing spousal support reads:

c. Upon entry of a judgment of divorce or separate maintenance, if the estate and effects awarded to either party are insufficient for the suitable support and maintenance of either party and any children of the marriage who are committed to the care and custody of either party, the court may also award to either party the part of the real and personal estate of either party and spousal support out of the real and personal estate, to be paid to either party in gross or otherwise as the court considers just and reasonable, after considering the ability of either party to pay and the character and situation of the parties, and all the other circumstances of the case. (Michigan Compiled Laws Section 552.23)

Spousal support awards can compensate the spouse who has rendered services other than wage earning to the marriage (most commonly caring for children, or homemaking for the spouse who is out earning wages or advancing a career during the marriage) and allow that spouse to continue living a lifestyle similar to that enjoyed during the marriage. While this is the ultimate goal, in many cases it is not realistic; often both parties experience a decreased standard of living. Spousal support is also based on the premise that where one spouse sacrifices a career to enable the other spouse to advance, the spouse who has developed earning capacity because of the sacrifices of the other should share the resultant income for a period of time after the marriage ends.

When a long-term marriage ends, spousal support provides income to a former spouse who, due to years of financial dependence on the other, is without support unable to enjoy a comparable standard of living. Spousal support is most appropriate in cases of long-term marriages with a great disparity in earning power. Traditionally, spousal support was paid in cases where a woman was a stay-at-home mother, and the husband went out into the workforce to make a living. However, spousal support is now gender-blind, at least in theory.

There are three types of spousal support. The first, often called alimony in gross, is actually a means of property division payable through either a lump-sum award or fixed periodic payments. It is non-modifiable and not subject to contingencies such as death of the recipient. It is sometimes used to make a property settlement more manageable and tax deductible to the payor. Because the tax laws regarding property settlements and deductibility of spousal support awards are complex, if your attorney suggests an award of alimony in gross, have the judgment reviewed by a tax professional before it is entered--unless, of course, your attorney is a tax expert.

Permanent or long term spousal support is sometimes awarded in long-term marriages where there is great disparity in earning power or when one spouse is disabled. Even permanent spousal support most often ends when the parties retire, become eligible for Social Security and begin drawing pensions or other retirement benefits.

Courts more often grant shorter-term rehabilitative spousal support to give the payee spouse the opportunity to become more viable in the job market through enhanced job skills or further education. Rehabilitative spousal support can serve to help a spouse obtain full-time employment and self-sufficiency, to obtain a degree, and adjust to a lifestyle based on the new economic realities following divorce. If, for example, the parties have children in college or own an expensive home, temporary rehabilitative spousal support may be appropriate to bridge the gap until the home is sold, the children graduate from college, or living expenses are otherwise adjusted.

The Spousal Support Factors

Spousal support awards are based on 14 factors which are not contained in any statute, but are derived from case law. These include:

1. parties' past relations and conduct;
2. length of the marriage;
3. parties' ability to work;
4. source and amount of property awarded to the parties;

5. parties' ages;
6. ability to pay spousal support;
7. parties' present situation;
8. parties' needs;
9. parties' health;
10. prior standard of living of the parties and whether the parties support others;
11. parties' contributions to the joint estate;
12. a party's fault in causing the divorce;
13. how cohabitation affects a party's financial status; and
14. general principles of equity.

The trial court must consider any factor it deems relevant, including fault, which should not be given disproportionate weight. While many people express moral outrage at the idea of continuing to support a spouse who has been unfaithful or abusive, fault is not generally considered a complete bar to spousal support.

In some cases, spousal support is not awarded at the time of entry of judgment, but is reserved for a period of years. In this instance, a party can ask for spousal support if it becomes necessary at a later date. If spousal support is not specifically addressed in the judgment of divorce, it is left open. A judgment of divorce should either clearly award spousal support, bar it completely, or leave it open.

Spousal support can be modified based on changed circumstances unless the parties agree in the judgment that it is non-modifiable. Most judgments of divorce provide that spousal support will be payable for a set number of years, with the amount being modifiable based on a change of circumstances. Spousal support typically ends when the recipient marries or cohabitates with another person as an economic unit. Spousal support is generally taxable as income to the recipient and deductible by the payor. Spousal support provisions are contained in the judgment of divorce and a uniform spousal support order, which, like a child support order, can be the basis for garnishment of wages.

The court cannot make spousal support non-modifiable unless the parties expressly agree to do so. If you are considering doing this so that your spouse cannot come back to ask for an increase, proceed with caution. The non-modifiability provision will apply to both the payor and payee. There have been cases where the payor has opted for non-modifiable support, thinking he was protecting himself from an increase, without thinking about what would happen if his income decreased. Case law has held that even with a drastic change of circumstances such as job loss or a serious health condition, non-modifiable spousal support is just what it says: non-modifiable. Thus, both the payee and payor of spousal support should carefully consider all the ramifications of non-modifiable support before making it so.

Sometimes the judgment of divorce requires the payor of spousal support to secure the support obligation with a policy of life insurance naming the payee as beneficiary. Because the present value of a spousal support obligation decreases over time, the amount of coverage required may proportionately decrease as time passes. If the judgment of divorce requires the payor to carry life insurance for this purpose, the judgment should require the payor to periodically furnish proof of life insurance coverage.

Temporary Spousal Support

In many cases, one spouse is in need of temporary spousal support immediately upon filing for divorce. This may be the case when only one spouse is employed and the other has significant childcare responsibilities, making it difficult or impossible to work outside the home. In divorces with children, the stay-at-home spouse may be unable to pay the mortgage, utilities and taxes without help from the employed spouse. In such a case, that spouse's attorney may file a motion for temporary support, asking the judge to look at the relative incomes of the parties, the current living expenses and budget, as well as debt carried by the parties. In other cases, both parties may be working full-time, but one of them may require temporary support from the other due to debt, or expenses previously shouldered by both spouses during the marriage. An award of temporary spousal support entered early in the case may remain in place until the final judgment. The final spousal support award may differ from the temporary spousal support award. Temporary spousal support may be awarded even in short-term marriages if one party is unable to pay living expenses during the pendency of the divorce.

If you are struggling financially after separation, talk to your attorney about filing a motion for temporary spousal support early on. If this is done, the judge will look at the relative incomes of the parties and their living expenses. You may be required to testify concerning your current budget and income. These motions can be difficult for a court to decide, as in many cases, both parties are experiencing economic turmoil, with one asking for support and the other having no resources from which to pay it.

As in child support cases, the court may impute income to one of the parties. In doing so the court will look at the educational level and work history of the party and, if the judge feels that the person has unexercised earning power, the spousal support calculation may be based upon imputed income. This is commonly done when, for example, one spouse has a college degree, but has been a full-time homemaker for a while. The other spouse in such a case would argue that with the change in family structure, the stay-at-home spouse should go back to work, especially if the children are grown. In this case, the judge would look at what the previously stay-at-home spouse might realistically earn on an entry-level basis were she to return to the workforce, and base spousal support on that income.

Sometimes the judgment of divorce states that the court retains jurisdiction to award spousal support where, for example, one spouse fails to pay his or her share of a joint debt or does not follow through on a property settlement. If the judgment of divorce requires that Paul and Ann each pay half of the jointly held credit card, and for some reason Ann fails to pay her half, leaving Paul on the hook for the entire thing, the court might order spousal support payments to compensate Paul. Spousal support is in most cases non-dischargeable in bankruptcy. If you have marital debt, talk to your attorney about incorporating language in your judgment protecting you in the event your ex files bankruptcy.

CHAPTER 7

Negotiating a Settlement

> "Let us never negotiate out of fear. But
> let us never fear to negotiate."
> — JOHN F. KENNEDY

lients often ask me in the early stages of divorce whether I think their case is more likely to settle or proceed to trial. While it is difficult to predict this, I tell them that, as a general rule, cases with fewer assets and where custody is not at issue are most likely to settle, and those with complex asset valuations or custody determinations are much more likely to go to trial. However, the most important predictor of success in resolving cases outside of the courtroom is the attitudes and personalities of the parties. Sometimes I have an opportunity to meet both spouses early in the proceedings, and I sense a spirit of cooperation and mutual desire to move beyond the conflict and reach a practical resolution. In other cases, the parties cannot agree on what time to have a meeting, let alone settle on a custody arrangement for their children. Unfortunately, if you are in a divorce with a spouse who has no intention of settling, there is not much you can do to force a settlement. As discussed in Chapter 2, if you hope to settle your case outside of court, make this known to your attorney and strategize on how best to accomplish this.

It is never too early to begin thinking about settling a divorce case. In fact, it is possible to come up with a settlement agreement before the complaint for divorce is even filed. The greatest obstacle to doing this is lack of information. Therefore, encourage your attorney to perform discovery early in the case, rather than waiting until just before the settlement conference. Nothing is more frustrating than appearing at a settlement conference, ready to negotiate, and having the attorney on the other side refuse to do so because of lack of information. If you are up to the task, you should prepare a complete spreadsheet of assets and debts, as well as a comprehensive summary of incomes for you and your spouse so that when the time comes to settle, all the numbers will be available.

I have used several different approaches to settle divorce cases. In the most amicable situation, I instruct my clients to sit down with the soon-to-be ex-spouse and prepare a joint spreadsheet of assets and liabilities. I caution my clients to hold off on signing this, and put a notation on it that it is **intended for settlement purposes only**. The Michigan Rules of Evidence provide that any document intended for settlement negotiations is not admissible at trial. This is important for both parties to understand. I have seen cases where the parties have sat down together early in the case without attorneys, negotiated a property settlement, reduced it to writing and signed it, only to have one attorney later say that the agreement is unenforceable, while the other attorney insists it is a binding settlement agreement, in spite of the fact that neither attorney was involved. A motion to enforce settlement has followed, and, in some cases, the court has enforced such a settlement. So, while I always encourage my clients to keep an open dialogue and attempt to resolve their disputes out of court, I caution them to clearly demarcate any written memorandum for settlement negotiation only and never to sign anything without providing it to me for review in advance.

Assuming that the joint spreadsheet exercise is fruitful, once I receive this preliminary document from my client, I will review the settlement, and if it is equitable, I will incorporate the terms into a proposed consent judgment of divorce for my client's eyes only as a template for settlement discussions. Sometimes a client fails to consider all the ramifications of a settlement until it is on paper and we have reviewed it together. For instance, clients often assume that if their soon-to-be ex-spouse agrees to assume and pay the mortgage on the marital home, only the spouse assuming the mortgage will be liable on the mortgage. When we actually discuss this provision, clients begin to understand that from the bank's perspective, both parties are still liable on the mortgage. They also begin to contemplate what it would be like to be liable on a mortgage for a house they no longer own, as their debt to income ratio will continue to reflect the liability on the mortgage, even if the other party pays it every month. This often overlooked aspect of settlements regarding real property is a virtual landmine for people trying to settle a case without an attorney.

Once I have incorporated the proposed agreement into a draft judgment of divorce, I carefully review it with my client, and if we agree that the settlement is equitable, I then provide a copy of the proposed judgment to opposing counsel. Once again, I will carefully note "for settlement negotiations only" on the proposed judgment. This exercise results either in a complete settlement or further negotiation. Whatever the result, I find this technique helpful in allowing both sides to envision the potential settlement and keep discussions moving forward. The ethical rules for attorneys provide that an attorney is obligated to communicate any settlement proposals to the client. If I do not hear anything from opposing counsel within a week or two after sending a proposed consent judgment, I will follow up with a phone call.

Clients sometimes ask me if there is a point of no return when it comes to settling a case, to which I reply no. Remember, the judge probably wants a case to settle just like the litigants do. In most counties, the court docket is crowded, and the judges would rather assist the parties in resolving a case instead of consuming a full day or more with a trial. However, the longer litigation proceeds, the more parties tend to become deeply entrenched in their positions. In order to prepare for trial, your attorney will spend considerable time subpoenaing witnesses, preparing exhibits, and studying your case. Trial witnesses such as accountants, psychologists or counselors may charge $1000 per day or more to block off their schedules for a trial. When the parties are indebted to the attorneys, they may look to one another for reimbursement of attorney fees, adding another point of disagreement to the mix. In spite of all this, try to keep an open mind regarding settlement right up until trial, for once parties arrive at the courthouse and understand all that is at stake, they tend to dig deeper than they would have in the comfort of their attorneys' offices, and settlement just happens.

Quite often, divorce cases are resolved at the settlement conference when the court sets aside time to explore whether a case can be settled. This meeting may take place about four to six months after the complaint for divorce has been filed in cases with children, and two or three months after filing in those without children. While the timeline varies between counties, most will schedule a settlement conference a month or two before the trial to explore settlement possibilities. In some counties, the court does not assign a trial date until after the settlement conference if the case has not settled.

While judges' practices vary widely regarding settlement conferences, most participate to some degree. The settlement conference may be a disappointing experience if the judge does not participate and merely has the attorneys meet in the hallway or conference room before giving them a trial date. If the judge is available and inclined to participate, he or she will often call the attorneys, without clients, into chambers for discussion. Sometimes my clients find this a bit disconcerting and wonder why they are left to pass the time in the courthouse hallway while the attorneys convene behind closed doors to discuss their case. Most of the time, judges will do this in order to get a candid assessment from the attorneys of the relative strengths and weaknesses of the case, and identify issues to be addressed at trial and the amount of time it will take.

If issues are contested, the attorneys will most likely bring those to the judge's attention in chambers at the settlement conference. For instance, if the dispute concerns spousal support, the attorneys will try to gauge the judge's informal opinion of their relative positions. Most of the time in a spousal support case, the judge will ask the attorneys about the nature of the marriage, as well as the incomes and expenses of the parties, and the attorneys and the judge will review the spousal support guidelines. Many times the judge will give an informal assessment of the issue. The attorneys can take this invaluable piece of information back to the clients to allow them to make an educated choice regarding settlement or trial. While it is inappropriate for a judge to render a ruling without hearing all of the evidence, sometimes the attorneys can pick up on the judge's attitude toward the respective positions of the parties and predict with some accuracy what the outcome might be at trial. With this additional information, the parties often move closer to settlement, as they are better able to assess the risks they face if they proceed to trial.

The settlement conference also presents an opportunity to discuss the judge's predisposition on custody. Where there has been a custody evaluation, the attorneys can assess whether the judge is inclined to follow or depart from it. Sometimes the custody investigator will provide input to the attorneys and the judge in an effort to resolve custody at the pretrial conference.

A settlement conference may consume the better part of the day. Sometimes a number of issues are settled, while others are reserved for trial. This allows the court to more accurately allocate the time necessary for the trial.

In some counties, rather than scheduling a formal settlement conference, the court schedules two or more trials for the same day, when everyone is expected to show up ready and able to try the case if the other cases scheduled on the same day settle at the last minute. This type of docket can be especially frustrating for clients who are are taking time off work, paying their attorneys to be present, and often paying for witnesses to hang out at the courthouse waiting for the case to be called. Often the older cases or those involving custody are given priority, leaving the parties and their attorneys on the lower priority cases to pass time in the courthouse hallway, sometimes for hours on end. This is not always a bad thing, though, as many cases tend to settle while the parties are waiting in the courthouse hallway. If your attorney uses the time productively, you will continue to engage in settlement discussions. I tell my clients to never give up on settling a case. This can happen early in the proceedings, at the settlement conference, or on the first day of trial. I have even seen cases settle after the first day of trial before the judge makes a decision. It is never too late. I strongly believe that settling is highly preferable to trial.

Here are the five most significant reasons that a settlement is better than a trial:

- A settlement is a voluntary agreement. Unlike a trial judge's decision, a settlement agreement is crafted by the people directly affected by it. Therefore, it is more likely to be in keeping with the parties' values, lifestyles, and individual needs. While most judges do a good job of considering these things, nobody understands the intricacies of your life better than you.

- A settlement will avoid the damage to your relationship that a trial inevitably causes. This is most important if you and your spouse have minor children. Settling your case sets a positive example for your children, and avoids having to air your grievances against one another in a public forum.

- A settlement avoids the expense of litigation. A full day trial, with two attorneys participating at $300 per hour, costs $4800, not including the cost of preparation, witness fees, subpoena expense, etc. I often ask my clients to envision this money placed in a tax-deferred college or savings plan for their children. I have heard some attorneys say they advise their clients that they would rather see the clients send their own children, rather than the attorneys' children, to college.

- A settlement can lessen the need to return to court repeatedly. In many cases, a trial cannot be completed in half a day or even a full day. Sometimes when I arrive at the courthouse ready to try a case, one or more people in orange jumpsuits are sitting in the courtroom waiting to be arraigned. Criminal cases take priority, and will pop up at a moment's notice. The court's docket is frequently interrupted by matters of greater priority. Remember, just because you have a trial date on the book does not mean your trial will be completed that day. You may have a partial trial and wait two or three months for another opportunity to state your case before the judge.

- A settlement is final. If you have a trial, there is always the possibility that someone will file an appeal, which can delay the process for months, a year or more.

Making it Final: Entry of Judgment

If you are fortunate enough to resolve your case at the settlement conference or earlier, you will still need to go to court for a final hearing, which your lawyer may refer to as a *pro con* (short for *pro confesso*, or by confession). If both parties and their attorneys have signed the judgment of divorce and any related support orders in advance of your *pro con* date, only one party, usually the plaintiff, and that party's attorney need to attend the *pro con*. The opposing party is welcome to attend, but in most instances it is not necessary and the hearing is quite brief. If you are the party presenting the proofs at the final hearing, you will be asked the following questions, or something similar:

- Is it true that you and [name of your spouse] were married on [date] in [county] in the state of [state]?
- Were there any children born of the marriage, and if so, what are their names and dates of birth?
- Is the wife currently pregnant?
- At the time you filed your complaint for divorce in this matter, were all of the allegations in the complaint true?
- Do the allegations in your complaint remain true today?
- Immediately prior to filing your complaint for divorce, had you (or the other party) been a resident of [county] for at least 10 days, and a resident of the state of Michigan for at least 180 days?
- Is it true that there has been a breakdown in the marriage relationship to the extent the objects of matrimony have been destroyed, and there remains no reasonable likelihood that the marriage can be preserved?
- Have you had an opportunity to review the terms of the judgment of divorce, and are you willing to be bound by them?
- Do you believe the property division in the judgment is fair and equitable?
- Are you asking the court to grant your judgment of divorce today?
- Do you believe the custody and parenting time provisions in the judgment of divorce are in the best interest of your children? (If minor children are involved)

- Are you and the other parent able to generally agree on important decisions regarding the upbringing of your child, such as medical, educational, financial and religious? (If minor children are involved and the judgment provides for joint legal custody)
- Why do you believe there has been a breakdown of the marriage and why should the divorce be granted? (The statute does not require this but sometimes a judge will ask. Rarely does a judge ask for any details, and I instruct my clients that if they are not inclined to share their life story, they can simply say that they and their spouse have grown apart or do not get along. Some clients, on the other hand, prefer to testify concerning the details of the marriage, which in my opinion serves no real purpose other than emotional venting. I do not encourage this.)

In most cases, after the plaintiff has testified, the court will confirm that it has jurisdiction over the matter and that the statutory standard has been met, and a divorce will be granted.

As discussed above, the divorce statute sets a waiting period of 60 days in divorces without children, and if minor children are involved, the waiting period is 6 months. The statute authorizes the court to shorten the waiting period if the parties present a compelling reason to do so. Some judges require nothing more than testimony that the parties have been separated for a period of time and agree it would be in the best interest of the children to finalize the divorce and move on. Other judges are more inclined to strictly adhere to the statutory waiting period. Ask your attorney how the judge in your case views such requests.

Once the court has confirmed that it has jurisdiction and the testimony of one of the parties establishes that the standard for granting the divorce has been met, the judge may sign the judgment immediately. The divorce is final when the judgment is signed. In most counties, one of the parties or attorneys can then take the judgment to the clerk's office, pay the judgment fee, and obtain a copy of the judgment on the spot. Your attorney may need to submit the judgment and uniform child support order at a later date, depending on local procedure. The judgment fee in Michigan is currently $80 and must be paid on or before entry of the judgment. Many counties now require payment of the fee at the time the complaint for divorce is filed. Confirm with your attorney's office in advance that this fee has been paid or be prepared to pay it at the time of the hearing. Many counties do not accept personal checks, so to be on the safe side, be prepared to pay with cash or a debit or credit card.

Mediation: The Positive Alternative

Most Michigan counties now refer divorce cases to facilitative mediation. This can be a highly effective process, especially if begun in the early stages of divorce, sometimes even prior to filing the complaint. Mediation is voluntary and requires that both parties meet with a neutral mediator to work cooperatively toward a mutually agreed settlement. In facilitative mediation, the most common type of alternative dispute resolution, the mediator does not act as a judge and does not render a decision or make any recommendation. Instead, the mediator's job is to maintain complete neutrality while encouraging the parties to move toward a settlement rather than going to court.

While mediation is generally ordered by the court, in most counties it is voluntary. In other words, if you attend a mediation, even by court order, no one will force you to settle your case through the process. While mediation is generally effective, it does not resolve all cases.

Some disputes are not suitable for mediation. Where there has been domestic violence, one of the parties may be fearful of or intimidated by the other. Mediation may not work in these cases, as the process is premised on an equality of bargaining power and open, honest communication. While cases with domestic violence can be resolved through mediation, it often requires additional work. If the parties are not allowed in the same room because of a restraining order, the process is more cumbersome and time-consuming, but may still be worthwhile. The courts require the mediator to screen the case for domestic violence to determine if it is suitable for mediation. In most counties, if this domestic violence screening form reveals existence of domestic violence, threats or intimidation between the parties, the court must conduct a hearing regarding suitability for mediation.

I can usually tell after one meeting with the parties whether the case is likely to be resolved at mediation. Though at the start of mediation few people feel confident that their case can be resolved without a trial, I find that once they sit down at a table with a good mediator, they begin to realize they have the power to resolve their dispute.

One predictor of success at mediation is the relative positions of the parties as expressed at the initial meeting. If they see the dispute as an all-or-nothing proposition, mediation is less likely to succeed, as it is based on a spirit of compromise and requires each party to give a little ground and meet in the middle. If I sense that one party is dead set on adhering to unreasonable expectations I might not recommend mediation. An example would be a custody case where one party feels the other parent should have no contact with the children. While this may be the outcome in the most extreme cases, as in situations of severe abuse or neglect, there will nearly always be some parenting time provided for both parents, as the law presumes that children have a right to a close relationship with both parents.

At mediation, the parties meet with an individual skilled in dispute resolution, often a family law attorney, a mental health professional or a business person. Michigan now requires mediators appointed by the court to complete a 40-hour domestic relations mediation training course, as well as observation of a few mediation sessions for certification. However, parties can choose most anyone they trust and agree upon to act as a mediator.

Mediation is most often conducted a few weeks into the divorce process, after there have been some negotiations. The court may have already entered temporary custody and support orders. Often both parties are represented by counsel, and the attorneys appear at the mediation. Attorney participation can be helpful, provided the lawyers recognize their role in mediation is that of legal advisor and not so much an adversary.

Because mediation is a confidential settlement negotiation, nothing said or produced there is admissible as evidence in court. This gives the parties freedom to discuss their positions and explore possible solutions without fear that something they say can come back to haunt them if mediation is unsuccessful and the case ends up going to trial. Neither party can call the mediator as a witness at trial. There are exceptions to the confidentiality rule in cases of abuse, neglect or criminal behavior. If the mediator learns of this, he or she may be obligated under the law to report it.

Early stage mediation may take place when the parties have not yet hired attorneys but have decided that they are ready to divorce and want to avoid the adversarial trial process. They may be unable to afford attorneys and may desire to resolve their disputes in a more cooperative setting. Pre-filing mediation can be effective, especially if the mediator is well-versed in domestic relations law. While the mediator cannot give legal advice and must maintain neutrality, he or she can provide information, such as a review of the child custody factors or calculation of child support under the Michigan Child Support Formula. If the parties are successful in resolving a case through early stage mediation, they can work with an independent lawyer who can prepare a judgment of divorce based on the settlement agreement. Ideally, both parties will have attorneys review the settlement agreement before it is incorporated into a judgment of divorce.

Most attorneys feel it is unethical for an attorney to represent both husband and wife in a divorce. If the mediator refers the matter to an attorney for preparation of the judgment of divorce after mediation, that attorney may act on behalf of one party or the other and recommend that the opposing party retain his or her own attorney to review the judgment once it is prepared. While this may cost a few hundred dollars, the peace of mind that will result from both parties having their own counsel is well worth the investment.

Mediation can be formal or relaxed, depending on the mindset of the parties and the style of the mediator. Ideally, they will submit financial, asset and debt information, as well as information on the parties' proposed parenting schedules and the children's needs in advance of mediation. This may be done through a questionnaire or by meeting with the parties. With late stage mediation, the parties may have previously prepared asset spreadsheets for their attorneys, which can be provided to the mediator. The mediator should have the parties sign an agreement regarding fees, the mediation process in general, and confidentiality.

Some mediators prefer to conduct a conference call in advance to discuss general procedures for mediation, fees, and confidentiality. If attorneys are involved, the mediator may ask them to participate in the initial conference. Attorneys can be very helpful at mediation if they recognize that the process belongs to the clients and do not try to take over. The mediator will encourage the parties to do their own talking, in order to instill a sense of ownership in the process.

At the first mediation session, the mediator will gather all necessary information and in many cases ask the parties to make an opening statement. The mediator may ask open-ended questions in order to facilitate discussion gain an understanding of the parties' expectations for mediation and their respective positions. If the parties' positions are diametrically opposed, the mediator may start by trying to find common ground. For instance, if both husband and wife come to the mediation saying they want sole custody of the children, the mediator may begin by defining interests and common goals and placing the focus on the child's needs, rather than focusing on positions. If the mediator can assist the parties in coming to an agreement on some basic principles, for example, that they are both ultimately concerned about the safety and well-being of the children, things can begin to move in a positive direction.

Mediation should be solution-focused, rather than a time to air grievances. I have found as a mediator, though, that some people want to use it as a platform to speak their mind, which in some cases can help people get things off their chests and move the process forward. Some mediators will tolerate or even encourage emotional venting, while others are quite uncomfortable with it. I have seen instances where, after one of the parties voiced hurt and anger to the other over past conflicts, they exchanged heartfelt apologies, which allowed them to put aside their hurts and move forward with a solution they both felt was in the best interest of the children. Other times, when the parties have tried to address their hurt and frustration, it has led only to escalating argument and resulted in a failed mediation. Each case is different, and whether emotional issues are explored at mediation will depend largely on the comfort level of the mediator and the parties. In some cases, it is best for the parties to discuss emotionally charged issues with a counselor, allowing mediation to remain focused on solutions.

Mediation may prove successful in resolving some, but not all, of the issues in a case. If this is the result, the mediator can put together a partial settlement agreement and report to the court which issues remain unresolved. While people usually prefer to reach a complete resolution, if that does not happen, a partial resolution can help define the issues for trial and assist the parties and the court in focusing on those issues worthy of the court's time.

In some cases, mediation takes place over a series of meetings that can extend for weeks or even months. In cases with a variety of assets, business interests, or debts, information gathering and valuation of assets can consume considerable time and require the involvement of third parties, such as business valuation experts or accountants. If the parents are working toward an agreement on custody and parenting time issues, they may need feedback from a counselor outside of mediation in order to explore the children's desires and needs before they feel comfortable reaching an agreement.

If a complete resolution is reached, there will be no need for a trial, but the plaintiff in all cases is required to go to court and request entry of a judgment of divorce in conformance with the mediation agreement.

The process described above, utilized in most domestic mediations, is facilitative mediation, in which the mediator makes no recommendation and maintains complete neutrality. In some cases, if the parties desire more guidance from the mediator in settling their dispute, a variation of the process, known as evaluative mediation, may work. In this process, the mediator participates in discussion and negotiation just as he would in facilitative mediation. However, the mediator will then offer an opinion or recommended settlement to the parties. Unless agreed in advance, this is nothing more than a recommendation, based on what the mediator perceives is fair and equitable and in line with what a judge might do were the case to proceed to trial. The parties can either accept or reject the evaluation.

A third type of alternative dispute resolution is binding arbitration. Through this process, the parties seek an order from the court appointing an arbitrator in advance of the proceeding. This person can be appointed by the judge or chosen by the parties. Most divorce arbitrators are attorneys experienced in domestic relations law. The attorneys may submit briefs, and the arbitrator will listen to testimony and receive exhibits just as a judge would at trial. The arbitrator then issues an opinion and order that is adopted by the court and incorporated into the terms of a judgment of divorce. The rules for domestic relations arbitration are governed by statute and court rule, and the procedure is more formal than mediation. The arbitration statute requires that portions of the hearing concerning child support, custody or parenting time must be on the record before a court reporter. The arbitration statute also contains detailed procedures for enforcement of arbitration awards, the filing of judgments, objections to the arbitrator's award, and other mandatory procedures. The arbitration rules can be found at Michigan Compiled Laws Sec. 600.570-582

If you are considering alternative dispute resolution as a means of resolving your divorce outside of court, talk to your attorney about which of the methods discussed above would be best suited for your case.

CHAPTER 8

When All Else Fails: Going To Trial

"Unfortunately, what many people forget is that judges are just lawyers in robes."
— TAMMY BRUCE

S o this is it. The day you have been waiting for, or possibly dreading. The day your divorce goes to trial. You have been through mediation and a settlement conference and, for one reason or another, your case has not settled. When you reach this stage, the only thing left to do is go to trial. This is the time when your attorney truly takes the lead and you place your fate in the hands of the court system. Not a pleasant thought for most of us, but sometimes a reality. While every court and judge does things a bit differently, there are certain things you can expect in most every divorce trial. This chapter is designed to give you a general overview of the trial process.

To prepare for your day in court, your attorney will need updated financial information. If custody is at issue, she may ask you to sign authorizations to obtain updated school and medical records. Plan to take the whole day off, even if your trial is scheduled for a half day, as court often runs later than scheduled. While formal attire is not generally required in court, do your best to present favorably to the judge. If you have a suit or professional business outfit, wear it. If not, wear your best clean business casual attire. Remember to stand whenever the judge enters or leaves the courtroom, and if asked a question by the judge, always address him or her as "Your Honor." In most cases it is considered improper to directly address another person in court. If you have a question, present it to your attorney, who will direct it to the court. Unless the judge enters an order barring the public from your proceeding, anyone can be present in the courtroom as an observer.

Remember that your attorney's job is not only to present your case, but to listen carefully as your opponent, the judge or any witness is speaking. Keep a legal pad in front of you to take notes. If you have a question for your attorney, it is best not to verbalize it until after the witness is done speaking, as you do not want your attorney to be distracted from what is being said to answer your question. If you have a question, write it out on the legal pad and your attorney can review it and give it the attention it deserves at the appropriate time.

Divorces are not tried to a jury, so the judge decides all issues of law and fact. The attorneys must adhere to the Michigan Court Rules and Rules of Evidence in presenting their case. You can expect the judge to call the attorneys into chambers prior to starting the trial to discuss what issues need to be dealt with and what witnesses and exhibits may be introduced. This is often a last-ditch effort to settle your case, which is sometimes successful. Do not be surprised if your attorney emerges from the judge's chambers with a renewed settlement proposal, even if you had previously lost hope that your case would settle. I always encourage my clients to keep an open mind right up until the gavel falls, as many cases settle on the first day of trial with a bit of facilitation from the judge.

Sometimes the court needs to settle preliminary legal issues before the trial begins. For example, there may be legal arguments over admissibility of an exhibit, testimony of a witness or the order of presentation. These matters may consume significant time. Once they are resolved, the court will ask the attorneys for opening statements. These can be very brief, or rather lengthy, depending on your attorney's style. In most cases, the attorneys will begin by identifying what issues will addressed by the court, what witnesses will testify, and the desired outcome. In many divorce trials, the parties themselves are the only actual live witnesses who testify. In more complicated trials such as those involving assets of substantial value, the attorneys may need to introduce extensive documentation such as appraisals, account statements, evidence of cash flow and spending, real estate title documents, and business records. This can be a tedious process that can consume hours or even days. If the attorneys are working together cooperatively, they may agree to stipulate to certain facts in lieu of introducing exhibits and testimony from witnesses.

Testimony at trial is always presented in question and answer format, so that each time an attorney asks a question, the judge and opposing counsel can anticipate what evidence the attorney intends to introduce by hearing each question before the answer is actually spoken. Only relevant evidence is admissible in court. Relevant evidence is something that tends to shed light on a particular issue in the case and serves a legitimate purpose in getting to the bottom of the dispute. In addition, evidence must be trustworthy. For this reason, hearsay is inadmissible. When preparing for trial, talk to your attorney about whether certain items of evidence constitute hearsay. For example, sometimes people believe that a letter from a physician or counselor should be admissible because it is in writing. However, note that even written documents may constitute hearsay. Hearsay is defined as an out-of-court statement made by someone for purposes of establishing a matter that is at issue in the proceeding. Our justice system requires that anyone testifying in court is subject to cross-examination. The writer of the letter, if he or she is not present at the proceeding, will not be subject to cross-examination, thus a document authored and submitted to the court without affording the opportunity for cross-examination may be subject to varying interpretations and therefore inadmissible under the hearsay rule. So do not plan to rely on written documents as evidence unless you submit them to your attorney well in advance of the trial, and ask if a witness should be subpoenaed who can testify consistent with statements in the document. It can be very frustrating to appear at trial with what you believe are admissible documents, only to have the judge bar them from the proceeding because you do not have a witness present to testify in support. The hearsay rules can be complicated, and there are many intricacies. Be sure to submit any documents you intend to rely on at trial to your attorney as he or she prepares for court.

If your case involves custody, the court will need to hear testimony on all the custody factors discussed above, which can be extremely time-consuming. Sometimes the judge will interview the children, if they are of sufficient age to express a reasonable preference on custody and parenting time. You will want to coordinate this with your attorney. Do not simply bring your children to court assuming they will be part of the proceeding. Often the judge will not actually interview the children until the end of the trial. Do not attempt to coach your children on what they will say to the judge when they are interviewed. Many judges and savvy custody investigators will start their interview by asking the child, "So what did your mother/father want you to tell me today?" In many cases, especially those involving younger children, this inquiry will reveal to the investigator immediately whether the children have been coached by a parent.

If you or your children have been counseling with a mental health professional, discuss with your attorney in advance of trial whether to subpoena the counselor. Some counselors are very reluctant to testify at trial and will do anything in their power to avoid it, including charging an hourly fee in accordance with time lost in professional practice. This is understandable, as a counselor will need to clear the entire schedule on the day of trial, which can result in financial loss unless reimbursed by the client. Although the law is somewhat unsettled in this area, most of the time when a counselor testifies concerning opinions or conclusions reached in counseling in the context of a custody dispute, those statements will be deemed expert testimony. For this reason, counselors, psychologists, or physicians who testify in a divorce matter will likely be permitted to charge an expert witness fee in line with what the witness would charge to see patients in the office setting. So if you anticipate involving anyone with professional expertise, be prepared to pay a substantial hourly fee that can rival or exceed that of your attorney.

The plaintiff, the person filing the complaint for divorce, will generally present his or her case first, with the defendant having an opportunity to present witnesses and exhibits in response. The court will hear testimony concerning custody, parenting time, child support, the incomes of the parties, the spousal support factors, personal property, including valuation and proposed distribution, and marital debts. Your attorney will probably file a pretrial summary or trial brief as a roadmap for the judge to understand the issues to be addressed in the trial. Be sure to ask your attorney to allow you to review this before it is filed to see that it addresses all of the issues from your perspective. Ask your attorney to allow you to review opposing counsel's trial brief, which will alert you to the opposition you will face at trial and allow you to better prepare.

If any issues in your divorce are contested, you will most likely testify. This can be a stressful event, even for those with courtroom experience. While it is difficult to anticipate exactly what questions you will be asked at trial, here are a few pointers on testifying, regardless of the scope of inquiry. Some things to remember:

- Tell the truth. I cannot emphasize this one enough. You will be under oath as a witness at your divorce trial, and providing false testimony is a crime. This should go without saying. However, you would be surprised at how many people ask me if it is okay to bend the truth a bit in court. It is absolutely not okay, and if you are my client and insist on doing this, I will have no choice but to withdraw as your attorney.
- Listen carefully to the question, and answer only the question. Do not ramble or provide narrative testimony. If you can answer a question with a simple yes or no, that is best. It is not your job to win your case or explain all of your answers when you are being cross-examined by opposing counsel. It is the opposing attorney's job to elicit testimony from you that is damaging to your case and helpful to your spouse's case. You will say some things on cross-examination that you want to explain, and if your spouse's attorney is aggressive, he or she will not allow you to do that, leading you to feel backed into a corner. Your attorney should listen carefully to this testimony and then ask you questions on redirect examination that give you an opportunity to explain or qualify your previous answers. If you have been asked questions on cross-examination that make you feel uncomfortable or that you felt

were misleading, bring those to the attention of your attorney, and she can then ask questions to allow you to explain more fully.

- Do not argue with opposing counsel. You may feel that you are being attacked or tricked. Try to maintain your composure and do not raise your voice or allow your emotions to take over.

- Do not be afraid of pauses or periods of silence. Sometimes attorneys will ask a question best answered by a simple yes or no. After the answer is provided, the attorney stands and stares at the witness, sometimes for several seconds, as if to say, "Is that all?"—in an effort to make the witness believe he has not provided a complete or correct answer to the question. If you as a witness fall for this technique and change or supplement the answer, it can damage your credibility.

- Don't be afraid to say you don't know. If opposing counsel asks you, for example, "How much is owed on your home equity line of credit?" and you have no idea, do not be afraid to say "I don't know" and end it there, even if the attorney stands there in silence, staring you down. If you don't know something, the worst thing you can do is first to say you don't know, and then go into a long, rambling guessing game that serves no purpose other than to damage your credibility and confuse the judge.

- Keep an eye on your attorney while opposing counsel is asking you questions to see if there will be an objection. Let the attorneys finish their questioning before you start your answer. Your attorney may want to object, so do not jump the gun by providing an answer before your attorney has an opportunity to object. Don't be afraid of pauses or silence. If a question is asked, and your attorney stands or looks as though she is going to say something, pause for a minute and do not answer the question until you are sure your attorney is comfortable with it.

Often at the conclusion of a trial, the judge will take a break and in many cases may render a ruling from the bench. In more complicated matters, the judge may hear all of the testimony and closing arguments of counsel, and if issues of law remain to be decided, may request additional briefing from the attorneys. When this occurs, it may be days, or even weeks, until you know the outcome of your case.

Once the court has issued a ruling on all the important issues, the plaintiff's attorney is responsible for preparing a judgment of divorce which must be approved by all counsel and signed by the judge before your divorce can become final.

Remember, you are not actually divorced until the judge has signed the judgment of divorce and all related support orders. If temporary orders are in place regarding custody, parenting time, support, and property, you must abide by those until the final judgment is signed and served on all parties. There may be work to do after the divorce judgment has been signed. In most cases, one of the attorneys will need to prepare the necessary orders to finalize the division of retirement assets. You may need to exchange titles to automobiles, change beneficiaries on life and health insurance, and transfer rights in the marital property through a quitclaim deed. Be sure to ask your attorney about any paperwork necessary to carry out the terms of the divorce judgment. Most judgments of divorce will nullify any existing wills or trusts or other estate planning instruments. Remember to consult with your attorney regarding updates to your estate plan after the divorce.

We Can Always Appeal—Or Can We?

So what will happen if the court comes up with a ruling that is simply so unjust that you simply cannot live with it? If, for example, you look at the property distribution and conclude that it is so inequitable or unjust that it had to have been based upon a mistake of fact, can anything be done? Or perhaps the parenting time arrangement is so convoluted and unworkable that you believe it is contrary to the best interest of your children and will cause them serious emotional distress. There is a right of appeal in divorce cases but the process is not easy, and the standard of appeal is a tough one to meet.

Depending on whether your judgment of divorce was a result of a trial or a settlement and consent judgment, the court rules provide specific measures to address problems with the judgment, short of an actual appeal. If both parties agree, the court will in most cases readily accept a consent amendment to the judgment. If you note inconsistencies between the judgment and what you believe was agreed upon or ordered by the judge, bring these to your attorney's attention immediately, as problems with a judgment resulting from mere clerical error can be easily addressed. In some cases it is possible to file a motion for new trial if the court's ruling was based on mistake of fact or if there has been fraud upon the court by one of the parties. Do not wait to bring this to the attention of your attorney, as the court rules impose specific deadlines on filing motions for new trial, for relief from any aspect of the judgment, or to file an appeal.

Appeals in divorce cases are relatively uncommon due to the complexity and expense of the procedure and the fact that, as a general rule, the appellate courts, at least in custody cases, are reluctant to overturn the decision of a trial judge who has actually heard all of the evidence unless it can be shown that there was an abuse of discretion, a significant mistake of fact or clear error of law. If after exploring all options, including a motion for new trial, you feel that the court made a serious error in deciding the issues of your case, talk to your attorney about the appeal process. If your attorney does not have experience with appeals, find one who does, as this is a specialized and somewhat technical area of the law. While in some cases appeal is available as a matter of right, in other situations it is only by leave. In either situation, you can rest assured that the appeal process will be lengthy and expensive. While the appellate rules provide for expedited hearings in custody cases, it may still take several months for the court to render a decision after the briefs are filed and arguments are heard.

CHAPTER 9

Domestic Violence

"In violence, we forget who we are."
— SOURCE UNKNOWN

omestic violence in a marriage greatly changes the dynamics in divorce. The imbalance of power occasioned by domestic violence can make negotiation or mediation impossible, and the emotional effects on the victim may include clouded judgment or irrational behavior.

The National Coalition Against Domestic Violence defines domestic violence as "the willful intimidation, physical assault, battery, sexual assault, and/ or other abusive behavior as part of a systematic pattern of power and control perpetrated by one intimate partner against another." Michigan's state standards for batterer intervention programs define domestic violence as "a pattern of controlling behaviors, some of which are criminal, that includes but is not limited to physical assaults, sexual assaults, emotional abuse, isolation, economic coercion, threats, stalking and intimidation. These behaviors are used by the batterer in an effort to control the intimate partner. The behavior may be directed at others with the effect of controlling the intimate partner" (http://www.biscmi.org/aboutus).

Michigan's domestic assault law applies to assaults committed against persons who are or were in domestic (dating, marriage, family or having a child in common) relationships with the defendant (Michigan Compiled Laws Section 750.81).

Domestic assault and domestic assault and battery are misdemeanors punishable by up to 93 days in jail and a $500 fine. If the person has prior convictions for domestic violence crimes, the penalties are more severe.

Personal Protection Orders

The primary means of legal protection against domestic violence is a personal protection order issued by the circuit court. A person seeking protection from domestic violence may file a petition with a circuit court's family division, requesting that the court grant a personal protection order against a current or former spouse, an individual with whom the person has a child in common, an individual with whom the person is or was in a dating relationship, or a current or former resident of the person's household. There is no filing fee for such a request, and application forms are available through the clerk's office at the family division of most circuit courts. Complete instructions and all forms are also available online through the Michigan Courts website: www.Courts. Mi.gov/Administration/SCAO/Forms/courtforms/Personalprotectionorder.

A person may request an *ex parte* personal protection order, in which the petitioner (the person filing the petition) asks the court to issue an order without holding a hearing or otherwise notifying the respondent (the person from whom the petitioner seeks protection) that the petition has been filed.

A judge will grant an *ex parte* personal protection order if the petitioner's affidavit shows that immediate and irreparable injury, loss, or damage will result from the delay caused by the time it takes to notify the respondent of the petition, or from adverse actions taken upon notification of the petition. If the order is granted, the respondent may object to the order within 14 days after being served with it. When that occurs, the court must conduct a hearing to determine if the order should remain in place. In some cases the court will initially refuse to grant a request for *ex parte* order, requiring that a hearing first be held. This may happen in cases where, although the petition raises valid concerns, the judge for any reason is not convinced that the relief sought in the petition must be granted before giving notice and an opportunity to be heard to the responding party.

A personal protection order may contain any or all of the following prohibitions against the respondent:

- entering the premises
- attacking, wounding, molesting or beating a named individual
- threatening to kill or injure a named individual
- removing a minor child from the person who has legal custody
- having access to records of the petitioner and respondent's minor child that disclose the petitioner and child's telephone number or address or the petitioner's employment address
- purchasing or possessing a firearm
- interfering with the petitioner's attempts to remove the minor child or personal property from premises solely owned or leased by the respondent
- interfering with the petitioner at the petitioner's workplace or school
- engaging in conduct that constitutes stalking or aggravated stalking
- interfering with the petitioner at the petitioner's workplace or school or engaging in conduct that interferes with the petitioner's employment or education
- any other conduct that interferes with the petitioner's personal liberty or causes the petitioner to reasonably fear violence
- any other act or conduct specified by the judge in the order.

A person arrested for violating the terms of a personal protection order may be charged with criminal contempt. If convicted, the person may be sentenced up to 93 days in jail and fined $500. (Michigan Compiled Laws §§ 764.15a, 764.15b)

Parties in a divorce frequently seek personal protection orders, as the threat of domestic violence may increase when the victim is attempting to end the relationship. However, judges may look with greater scrutiny on petitions for personal protection orders filed during divorce proceedings, as they can be misused by parties jockeying for more control of the children in a custody dispute or as an effort to exclude the other parent from the marital home. Before filing a petition for personal protection order in the context of a divorce proceeding, consult with your attorney and consider if the remedies available in the divorce proceeding itself are adequate to address the situation. If you are seeking to exclude your spouse from the marital home simply because of increased stress or arguing in the presence of the children, it may be appropriate to pursue exclusive possession of the marital home through a motion in the context of the divorce proceeding, and not through a petition for personal protection order. If you foresee a custody dispute, I would advise against filing a petition for personal protection order to exclude the other parent from the marital home solely in an effort to gain an advantage in the custody determination. Judges and custody evaluators will in most cases see right through this strategy and it will ultimately do more harm than good to your custody case. **However, safety is of paramount concern, and if you have any reason to believe that you or your children are in danger, do not hesitate to file a petition for personal protection order immediately.**

When you obtain the personal protection order petition form, tell the clerk you are seeking a domestic personal protection order. In most cases the judge will act promptly and either grant or deny the petition or schedule a hearing. The statute requires that the hearing, if required, be held within 21 days. If the judge enters the order, it must be served on the respondent to be effective against him or her. The forms contain specific instructions on how to effect legal service of the order. Remember, you cannot serve the PPO yourself.

Once the court enters a personal protection order and you have had it served, the respondent may file an objection and motion to modify or terminate the order. If this occurs the court will conduct an evidentiary hearing where the petitioner has the burden of proving, through his or her own testimony and that of any pertinent witnesses, that the order is necessary to prevent the respondent from engaging in any conduct prohibited by the order.

Keep in mind some practical considerations concerning personal protection orders. First, a petition for personal protection order is a separate proceeding from the divorce case and will be assigned a separate case number ending in PP. If you have an attorney in your divorce case, do not assume he or she will receive copies of the petition for personal protection order. If you desire the assistance of an attorney in the personal protection order proceeding, the attorney must file an appearance in the case. Most divorce attorneys require a separate retention agreement and often an additional retainer to appear in personal protection proceedings. If you file a petition for personal protection order, let your divorce attorney know immediately. Sometimes, given the urgency of the situation, a petitioner does not have time to consult with an attorney prior to filing the petition. If you believe that you are in danger, consulting with your attorney may have to wait. However, do not delay bringing the matter to your attorney's attention as soon as practicable.

Second, keep in mind that a personal protection order is a court order that must be followed by both the petitioner and the respondent. If the order prohibits the respondent from coming to your home or calling you on the telephone, do not initiate or allow such contact, even if you believe the situation has improved. This will seriously damage your credibility if things deteriorate once again and you find yourself in a hearing to determine whether the personal protection order should be dismissed. If you do not honor your own order, or by your actions encourage the other party to violate it, the court may be less inclined to take your situation seriously, and the judge may set aside the order on request of the respondent.

Third, remember that personal protection orders last for a minimum of 182 days unless a different time is set by the court. The order must state the date of expiration on its face. Unless a petition to extend the order is filed, the order will expire by its own terms. Keep track of the date of expiration, and if you believe extension of the order is appropriate, be sure to file a petition to extend the order well in advance of the date of expiration.

Most importantly, remember that while a personal protection order is enforceable anywhere in Michigan and is the best protection the law affords, it is not a guarantee of personal safety. If you have reason to believe that someone will cause harm to you or your children in spite of any court order, do not hesitate to speak with law enforcement, your attorney, or a representative of a local domestic violence organization to discuss what additional measures you may need to take for your personal safety.

CHAPTER 10

Moving On: After the Judgment of Divorce is Entered

> "Peace is not absence of conflict; it is the ability
> to handle conflict by peaceful means."
> — RONALD REAGAN

Once the court has entered the judgment of divorce, it may take a few weeks for the final paperwork such as real estate deeds, vehicle titles, and qualified domestic relations orders, if necessary, to be signed and processed. In some cases, the court will need to address matters that arise after the judgment of divorce is entered. The most common post-judgment proceedings involve property enforcement, modification of parenting time or custody, change of domicile of the children and modification of support based on changed circumstances. After a divorce judgment has entered, the court retains jurisdiction to address all of these issues.

If you think you might need assistance with post-judgment matters, discuss this with your attorney at or before your final divorce hearing. Most judgments of divorce discharge counsel of record, and your attorney may require a new fee agreement and retainer for post-judgment proceedings.

Enforcement of Property Provisions in the Judgment of Divorce

Most people understand that the judgment of divorce is binding and compels them to do certain things regarding the transfer of property, payment of debts, etc. However, whether intentionally or through simple neglect, people sometimes fail to do what the judgment of divorce requires, necessitating a return to court. Some grounds for post- judgment enforcement motions include failure to transfer real estate deeds or vehicle titles, failing to pay debts or a sum payment in equalization of the marital estate as required under the judgment, and inability or refusal to refinance a mortgage on real property.

If your ex does not comply with the judgment of divorce, talk to your attorney about filing a post-judgment motion. Most judgments of divorce contain a provision stating that, if a party fails to comply with the conditions of the judgment, he or she may be ordered to pay the other party's resultant attorney fees.

One of the most serious compliance issues is failure of the spouse who retains the marital home to apply for and obtain a new mortgage on the home. This is a real problem in cases where the other spouse has relinquished her ownership in the home, but remains liable on the mortgage. In some cases, this can prevent a person from qualifying for a new mortgage, as it affects the debt-to-income ratio. Before your judgment is entered, talk to your attorney about incorporating a provision requiring the marital home to be sold if it is not refinanced within a certain time. This will give the party who takes ownership of the home an incentive to refinance promptly.

It is also a good idea to incorporate specific identifying information such as the legal description of any real estate, and the VIN for any vehicles or watercraft in the judgment of divorce. This may enable you to transfer title based on the judgment in the event your ex fails to sign over the deed or title.

In most cases, if one party does not comply with the judgment, especially if the failure is intentional, the court can modify the judgment to compensate the non-offending party through modification of spousal support or awarding additional assets. If you are forced to go to court following the divorce to enforce any aspect of the property division, request that your attorney file a motion for attorney fees.

Changes of Custody

Of the many post-judgment matters that may arise, a change of custody is perhaps the most significant. As discussed in chapter 4 above, the rule of law in custody cases is stability for the children. The courts do not readily change custody absent a significant change of circumstances. Even then, it is difficult to change custody for a number of reasons. Before even considering such a motion, the court will need to determine whether there is an established custodial environment with one or both parents. This threshold determination must be made in every custody proceeding. An established custodial environment will be found to exist with a parent if "over an appreciable period of time, the child naturally looks to the custodian in that environment for guidance, discipline, the necessities of life, and parental comfort" (Michigan Compiled Laws Section 722.27 (c)). The Child Custody Act further provides that where an established custodial environment exists the court shall not modify or amend a previous custody order unless there is presented clear and convincing evidence that the change is in the child's best interest. The clear and convincing evidence standard is a higher and therefore more difficult burden of proof than the usual preponderance of evidence standard.

If you are contemplating a motion for change of custody, discuss this with your attorney, as filing such a motion is no small task. You must first determine whether there has been a change in circumstances. Generally, passage of time in and of itself is not sufficient to constitute such a change. Most commonly, change in circumstance involves a physical relocation of one of the parties, remarriage or cohabitation by a parent, bad behavior by a parent such as substance abuse, criminal acts or other activities that may place the child in danger, a change in a party's physical or mental health, financial condition, housing or work schedule and any other development that may affect the child's well-being. What constitutes a change in circumstances is wide and varied. I have seen motions for change of custody that revolve around the child's pet allergy, a health condition of one of the parents, stress over blending of stepfamilies, and a host of other situations. Remember, even if the burden of showing a change in circumstances is met, if you are trying to change custody when there is an established custodial environment you must convince the court by the elevated evidentiary standard of clear and convincing evidence that such a change is in the best interest of the child. The law presumes that it is in a child's best interest to enjoy a close relationship with both parents. Therefore, changing custody from joint to sole or from one parent to the other is a challenging proposition.

Child custody determinations are particularly challenging when children reach their teenage years and begin to express a strong preference on where they spend their time. I am often asked whether teenagers are allowed to decide for themselves where they will live. While the courts must address this issue on a case-by-case basis, the law is clear that regardless of the age of the child, the court and the parents, and not the child, determine where the child will spend his or her time. Although one of the factors in the child custody act is the reasonable preference of the child, in changes of custody, the court must look at the totality of circumstances, and the child's preference is only one of many factors. As children grow older, they tend to spend less time with their parents and more with their peers. Their preference may evolve over time as they become involved in sports, begin dating, and become more independent, which can greatly complicate the custody determination.

In contemplating whether to file a motion for change of custody, ask your attorney whether he has had similar custody cases in the past. If your attorney has been litigating custody matters in front of the judge assigned to your divorce case, he can likely provide you with an opinion on the likelihood of succeeding on a change of custody motion. Remember, if there is an established custodial environment, when it comes to changing custody, you must prove by a heightened evidentiary standard that the change is in the best interest of the child.

Change of Parenting Time

If you are divorced when your children are young, chances are parenting time will change periodically as the children grow older. As in a motion to change custody, modifications in parenting time are based on changed circumstances and what is in the best interest of the child. The law requires that the court utilize the same twelve "best interest of the child" factors discussed in chapter 4 above. Some common reasons for changes of parenting time include changes in a child's schedule, distance considerations if a parent moves, change in schooling or sports programs, difficulties in acclimating to blending of families, the child's evolving preference to spend more time with one parent or the other, health concerns, differences in parenting styles, neglect or abuse by a parent or any combination of factors. In high-conflict cases, parents often file motions for changes in parenting time when they are unable to agree on such things as where the children will be picked up and dropped off for parenting time, who will feed them dinner on parenting time exchange days, or who will transport them to sporting events.

Most Michigan circuit courts utilize referee hearings for parenting time motions. In most counties, the referee is an attorney employed by the county. In smaller circuits, the referee may wear a number of hats, such as Friend of the Court or assistant prosecutor. The referee acts as a judge would in considering the motion. The parties must adhere to the rules of evidence in front of a referee, just as they would before a judge, and the referee is required to interpret the law and apply the same evidentiary standards. The most significant difference between a judicial hearing and one before a referee is that the referee is not authorized to enter orders, but can issue a recommended order which is not effective until signed by the judge. The law provides a 21-day objection period from the date the recommended order is served on the parties. If either party objects to the order, the court must schedule a *de novo* ("from the new") hearing before the judge. At this hearing the judge will conduct a new hearing from the beginning, as if the referee hearing never occurred. The primary advantage of a referee hearing is that in most counties the referee is more accessible than the judge, allowing the parties to more expeditiously schedule a hearing on a parenting time matter. However, because of the built-in objection period, it is possible for a party to object and cause a delay of weeks or even months. This can be a problem when it comes to motions regarding change of domicile or where a child will attend school. In some cases, the courts will allow such motions to be heard immediately by the judge to avoid unnecessary delays and hardship for the child or the parents.

Domicile and Residence of the Children

Michigan law requires that unless otherwise agreed by the parties, neither parent is allowed to move the residence of a child out of Michigan or to a point more than 100 miles away from the residence of the child at the time the initial order regarding residence of the child was made. In some cases, even a move of less than 100 miles can upset the custodial and parenting time arrangement, and in such cases, the party intending to move must seek a modification of parenting time that will allow the other parent to continue a relationship with the children. The court must consider several factors in deciding whether a move is justified. A parent must prove that the move has the capacity to improve the quality of life for both the child and the parent. The court will look at whether the moving parent is in compliance with previous parenting time orders and whether the move is inspired or motivated by a desire to frustrate the other's parenting time. Also relevant to the determination is whether the parent opposing the move is doing so for financial gain. The party seeking to move the residence of the child must show that there will be an opportunity for continued parenting time with the other parent, and that the parents can realistically comply with the new parenting time order. As with changes in custody and parenting time, the court must first and foremost consider the best interest of the child in determining whether a move is justified.

Joint Custody-Related Motions

As discussed in chapter 4 above, if you and your ex share joint legal custody of your children, each of you has the right to participate in important decisions affecting the welfare of the child. These decisions are many, and include such issues as where the child will attend school, religious training, and the need for medical procedures, including surgery, vaccinations, and dental and orthodontic care. Whether a child will participate in a particular sport, especially contact sports involving potential for injury and those that require significant parental time and financial outlay can be the subject of conflict between parents with joint legal custody. Disagreements about overseas or out- of -state travel, schooling, and other important issues may require hearings from time to time. Some judgments of divorce provide that the parents will mediate any issues regarding the children before filing a motion. A little planning ahead in this regard can head off a lot of conflict. If your attorney has been practicing family law for a few years, she will most likely have a bank of clauses in her divorce form file designed to address issues such as decision making for sports-related expenditures and medical, dental and orthodontic care. The more bases you can cover in your judgment of divorce, the less likely you will find yourself in court in the years following entry of judgment.

Parenting Time Violations and Complaints

A parent can file a parenting time complaint with the Friend of the Court if the other parent is not complying with the parenting time order. Situations commonly giving rise to parenting time complaints include tardiness picking up or returning the children, failing to provide necessary clothing, medication or other supplies for the child, neglecting the child during parenting time, the use of drugs or alcohol, exposing the children to unsavory social situations, failing to assist the children with homework or transport them to school or extracurricular activities, and the list goes on. The Michigan Friend of the Court Office and most counties publish parenting time guidelines with minimum expectations for parenting time. If possible, familiarize yourself with these and discuss them with your ex so you are on the same page with respect to the everyday aspects of parenting time. In the event you are unable to agree, it may be time to file a parenting time complaint with the Friend of the Court. Typically, this involves a written complaint to the assigned caseworker, after which the worker will notify the other parent of the problem and provide an opportunity to respond in writing. If the worker is not satisfied by this response, the Friend of the Court or the aggrieved party may schedule a hearing before the judge or referee in an effort to resolve the complaint. In cases of more serious or repeated violations of parenting time, after an evidentiary hearing on an order to show cause the judge may hold the offending party in contempt of court, and may impose a fine, makeup parenting time, or other sanctions up to and including incarceration. If a party is repeatedly found in violation of a court's parenting time order, on motion of the aggrieved party, the court may change parenting time or even modify custody.

In high-conflict cases, some courts utilize parenting time coordinators, often licensed mental health professionals, who specialize in mediating and resolving parenting time and custody disputes. This should be seen as a last resort, as it can be costly and cumbersome. However, where there is significant ongoing conflict between the parents, it may be the only way the court can take control of the situation and allow the children to enjoy a relationship with both parents. A parenting time coordinator acts as a neutral go-between in order to lessen the emotional exposure of the parents to one another and bring order to the situation. The parenting time coordinator can address issues such as transportation, meals, attendance at extracurricular activities, parties present during parenting time, and other day–to-day issues that can cause conflict between the parents. In conjunction with appointing a parenting time coordinator, the court may order the parties to co-parenting counseling with a mental health professional in an effort to repair the relationship for the benefit of the children.

If you experience repeated conflict with your ex over parenting time, consider mediating the issue. In some counties, the Friend of the Court will offer mediation services to resolve parenting time complaints. Many community dispute resolution centers will mediate parenting time disputes, which can be an effective means for resolving these conflicts outside of court.

Estrangement and Parental Alienation

After the divorce, particularly if conflict continues over property, support, custody or parenting time, the children may begin to experience feelings of confusion, ambivalence, anger and sadness, all of which may be directed at one or both parents. A child may feel that he must be loyal to one parent at the expense of the other, or that because of the raging conflict it is impossible to love both mother and father.

Much research and writing has been devoted to the topic of parental alienation. In the 1980s, some mental health and legal practitioners began to label a cluster of symptoms commonly seen in children of divorce as "parental alienation syndrome". While the effects of alienating behaviors by a parent are often identifiable and most certainly do affect the child's relationship with the other parent, the medical and legal communities do not currently recognize the emotional effects of alienating behaviors as a syndrome or disorder. So proceed with caution in dealing with any person who claims to be an expert in any such diagnosis or syndrome.

In no way am I trying to minimize the destructive impact alienating behaviors can have on a child's relationship with a parent. This all too common situation can cause significant emotional distress for a child and can make parenting time stressful or even impossible for a parent on the receiving end of alienating behaviors by the ex-spouse. The post-divorce years are rife with opportunity for a parent to foster negative feelings in the mind of an impressionable child toward an ex-spouse. Probing questions to the child, derogatory statements about the other parent in the presence of the child or negative postings on social media can serve to create feelings of confusion in the mind of a child that can make it difficult for the child to behave appropriately with the other parent or to express affection for fear of appearing disloyal.

In some cases, parental alienation is not at all subtle. A parent may openly and in the child's presence accuse the other of sexual or physical abuse or otherwise mistreating or neglecting the child. The parent may refer to the ex-spouse as lazy, mean, stupid, or having other unflattering attributes. A parent may state in the presence of the children that vacation or birthday presents are being eliminated due to the other parent's failure to pay child support. These are but a few examples of alienating behaviors.

While the effects of parental alienation are often readily apparent and easy to detect in a child, proving that the child's negative attitude toward one parent has been contributed to by behaviors or statements of the other often proves difficult. If after the divorce one of your children appears to be drifting away from you emotionally, as evidenced by a refusal or reluctance to spend time with you, sulking or complaining during parenting time, or making unreasonable demands, parental alienation may be at work. In these cases, it is imperative that the child be seen by a mental health professional proficient in recognizing whether a parent's alienating behaviors are causing emotional upset for the child and who can help the child work through the accompanying feelings in an effort to preserve the parent-child relationship. If with the help of a professional you are able to pinpoint the behaviors on the part of your ex-spouse that are contributing to your child's emotional distress, it may be appropriate to petition the court for a psychological evaluation of the other parent to document the impact of such damaging behaviors. If you are able to document that your former spouse, whether innocently or intentionally, has engaged in alienating behavior, it can be grounds for a change in custody or parenting time. If the court detects that the custodial parent is doing or saying things that are causing damage to the relationship between the child and the other parent, the court may order additional parenting time for the non-offending parent to remove the child from the alienating forces at work and allow for healing in the relationship. In addition, the court may order counseling or parenting classes for the offending parent in order to address the alienating behaviors. If the court finds that the alienating behaviors are severe, it may order that the at-fault parent should have only supervised parenting time to prevent further emotional damage to the child.

Modification of Child Support

Child support is modifiable on a showing of change of circumstances, the most common of which is a change in income of one or both parties. However, the

Michigan Child Support Formula establishes a minimum threshold for modification. In order to modify a current support payment, the modification must be in an amount exceeding 10% of the currently ordered support payment or $50 per month, whichever is greater. If you have experienced a change in your income such that modification would be in order, or if you suspect that your ex-spouse has experienced increased earnings, you can petition the court for review of support, or file a motion before the domestic relations referee to modify support.

A second reason support may be modified is when there is a change in parenting time resulting in a shift in overnights spent with each parent. When filing a motion to modify parenting time, ask the court to review income information at the same time in order to accurately calculate support based on the new parenting time order. Like parenting time motions, child support motions are usually heard by a domestic relations referee and can also be referred to private or Friend of the Court mediation.

Modification of Spousal Support

In most cases, spousal support is modifiable upon a change of circumstances. In some cases, the judgment provides for non-modifiable spousal support; however, this must be by agreement of the parties. The court does not have authority to order non-modifiable support unless the parties specifically agree to it. If the parties have agreed on non-modifiable spousal support, the waiver of modifiability must be specifically stated in the judgment of divorce, otherwise modifiability is presumed.

There are many reasons for modification of spousal support. If any of the spousal support factors discussed in chapter 6 above have changed, it may be time to file a motion to modify spousal support. The most common reasons for modification are cohabitation or marriage of the recipient (this is usually specifically stated in the spousal support order), reduction in the payor's income, retirement, layoffs, health concerns, inability to pay, inheritance or financial windfall by one of the parties, promotions or demotions, and a host of other situations that can change either party's financial outlook dramatically. Motions for modification of spousal support are heard by the judge. The party seeking modification of support must prove a change of circumstances by a preponderance of the evidence.

Working Toward Peace after the Divorce

It's finally over. Your attorney has delivered copies of the final judgment, support orders, and related documents to you and the legal proceedings are done. You may have moved out and purchased a new home by now, or perhaps you have come to the realization that you are going to be renting for a while. Regardless of your financial situation, one thing is clear: You have a lot of healing to do. The years immediately following divorce can be perilous for you and your children. In this time fraught with uncertainty, people sometimes wonder if they did the right thing or if they could have prevented the divorce had they just worked a little harder in counseling.

If you have children, young or grown, the greatest gift you can give them following the divorce is to work toward a peaceful and businesslike relationship with your former spouse.

If possible, find a divorce recovery group in your community where you and your children can receive support from others who have been through the process and remind you that you are not alone.

There will most likely be times when you need to resolve conflict with your ex, especially where you have children in common. If your community has a dispute resolution center be sure to explore mediation opportunities there so you can keep any future disputes out of court. In addition, keep in mind that the Friend of the Court can assist you in mediating parenting time or support concerns.

As stated above, establish and keep a relationship with a professional counselor to help you navigate the emotional highs and lows you will experience in the years following your divorce. Look for opportunities to reinvent yourself. Perhaps now is a good time to explore changes in your career, where you live, your spiritual practices or life goals. While divorce is exceedingly difficult, it can also represent a new beginning and freedom to explore all that the next chapter of your life has in store. As you embark on the next part of your journey, may you find prosperity, healing and peace.

Table of Authorities Cited

	Cite
Child Custody Act	MCL 722.21-722.31
Domestic Relations Arbitration Act	MCL 600.570-582
Domestic Violence	MCL 750.81
Violation of PPO penalties	MCL 764.15a
Michigan Rules of Professional Conduct	MRCP
Medical Marijuana Act	MCL 333.26423, 26424
Michigan Child Support Formula Manual	
No-Fault Divorce Statute	MCL 552.6
Obergefell v. Hodges,	U.S. Supreme Court June 26, 2015
Parenting Time and Support Enforcement Act	MCL 552.601-552.650
Personal Protection Orders	MCL 600.2950
Spousal Support	MCL 552.23

Index

Made in the USA
Lexington, KY
30 May 2017